# ANGER

## Managing The Volcano Within

LEAP Learning Empowerment & Achieving Potential

ISBN 978-93-81115-68-8
Revised Edition Copyrights @ One Point Six Technologies Private Limited, 2026

First published in 2011 by Leadstart
A brand of One Point Six Technologies Private Limited
Unit no. 26, Ground Floor, A1, Shram Safalya,
Wadala Truck Terminal Road, Near Post Office,
Antop Hill, Mumbai -400037.
Email:info@leadstartcorp.com
www.leadstartcorp.com

Marketed & Distributed in India by Unbound Script
2/41, Ansari Road, Darayaganj, Delhi - 110002

All rights reserved. No part of this publication may be reproduced, stored in or introduced into a retrieval system, or transmitted, in any form, or by any means (electronic, mechanical, photocopying, recording or otherwise) without the prior written permission of the publisher. Any person who does any unauthorised act in relation to this publication may be liable to criminal prosecution and civil claims for damages.

# EDITORS OF LEADSTART

The Editors of Leadstart are a team of passionate literary enthusiasts with a creative and progressive focus. Our team includes distinguished authors, researchers, contributors, in-house editors, and writing talent from around the world. Many literary projects require a diverse team rather than a single author to write or update the book. These projects often involve cases where the original author is unable to continue, whether because they are unavailable or no longer with us. Our work thus spans a range of content, from original writings to thoughtfully abridged classics, updated editions, and translations.

LEAP Learning Empowerment & Achieving Potential

# ABOUT THE LEAP SERIES

The LEAP series of books has been conceived as a tool of empowerment for every individual to achieve their full potential.

There are certain aspirations that every person in the world shares. We all want to be happy. We all want to lead fulfilling lives. We all want to find our soulmate. We all want a job we love doing. We all want good friends who will share our joy and sorrow. We all want to believe that there is a purpose to our lives.

While the commonality of these goals spans the globe, their achievement is entirely individual. Each person possesses a unique and mixed gift of strengths and weaknesses, special talents and handicaps. To focus our individual lives on all that is positive within us, all that is possible for us to do, to be and to achieve, we need to take conscious steps towards it. The empowerment of our lives is an individual pursuit. The decisions are yours. The action is yours. To do the very best with what one has been given – that is the ultimate achievement of a life well lived.

**You Are You**

First, we must recognise ourselves and accept our particular basket of capabilities. Nobody is the same. Nor is it necessary to be like someone else.

**Find Your Horizons**

Once we are at peace with the composition of our own individuality, we can set out to enhance our capabilities in order to achieve full potential as an individual. We can utilize all the teaching around us to stretch our talents to the fullest extent in order to achieve worthwhile goals.

**Cap The Leak**

Once we recognize our potential, we can work to minimize the influence and impact of our weak points in order to allow the strengths to shine in everything we do.

**Row Your Boat**

Every day is part of the journey. Sometimes you win the day. Sometimes the day is lost. But you keep rowing towards the shore, towards your goals. In India, it is called sadhana. That special power within you drives you to achieve what you have set yourself to do.

The **LEAP** series teaches methods of individual empowerment.

ꟸ

# CONTENTS

## PART IV: GUIDANCE, SUPPORT, AND GROWTH



## CONCLUSION

L E A P Learning Empowerment & Achieving Potential

# UNDERSTANDING ANGER

# 1

# DEFINING ANGER & THE ESSENCE OF ITS MANAGEMENT

Let's be real: everyone gets angry. It's normal, and it's human. But how we respond to that anger determines whether it leads to healing or harm. When anger feels like a runaway train, it can hurt both you and the people around you. From mild irritation to full-blown fury, anger comes in many forms. Some people go silent, others lash out, and a few become defensive or sarcastic.

Violent or abusive outbursts, however, are never acceptable. It is essential to manage these reactions with maturity because staying calm is not just about being polite; it is about protecting your mental and physical health. Bottling up your rage is also not a solution. Repressed anger only turns inward, creating stress, anxiety, and frustration. The smarter approach is to address what makes you angry and to build healthier ways to respond. If someone tends to explode, shout, or get abusive in difficult moments, it may be time to seek help. That is where anger management steps in. The first step is to admit that there is an issue. The second step is to identify the root cause and understand what is triggering your emotions. Counselling, one-on-one support, and group sessions can help you do this. They help you recognise your anger triggers and guide you toward taking responsibility for your reactions. The goal is not to blame others, but to understand yourself and make better choices.

Anger management gives you tools to deal with intense emotions without losing control. Accepting help is not always easy. Many people resist it because they see it as a punishment. In truth, it is an opportunity to grow. Unchecked anger can cost you relationships, jobs, and peace of mind. Learning to manage it helps you reclaim balance and self-respect.

We have all lost our cool at some point, whether by snapping at a friend, yelling in traffic, or reacting harshly over something small. But when anger begins to control you instead of the other way around, the consequences can be destructive even if nothing physical is broken. The damage might be emotional, mental, or relational.

Uncontrolled anger affects your body, too. It raises your heart rate, floods your system with stress hormones, and puts your body in constant fight-or-flight mode. Over time, this takes a toll on your health, affecting sleep, digestion, and immunity. Physically and emotionally, rage can pull you backwards. While teens and young adults tend to struggle the most, since they are still learning emotional control, anyone can develop better anger management skills at any age. If you ever feel like you are on the edge, talk to someone you trust: a parent, teacher, friend, or counsellor. You are not alone, and reaching out for help is a sign of strength.

When you feel the pressure building, try a few quick ways to cool down:

- Step away from the situation and take a break.
- Punch a pillow or a punching bag, not a person.
- Draw your feelings on paper.
- Write in a journal until the emotion feels lighter.
- Exercise, run, or clean with focus and energy.

These methods will not solve the root cause immediately, but they can reduce the intensity long enough for your logic and self-control to return. Some people blame others for their anger. Others recognise their patterns and start making changes. Anger management is about learning to respond to difficult emotions, like hurt, jealousy, embarrassment, fear, or frustration, in healthier, more mature ways. Everyone's anger looks different. Some shout, some sulk, others go silent. The most dangerous kind is abusive anger, and that requires immediate attention and professional help.

Managing anger is vital for your emotional and mental health. It helps you stay calm, kind, and in control, rather than letting fury take over. That is what anger management programs are built around: giving people the tools to understand their feelings, make better choices, and build more peaceful lives.

The first step is ownership. Admitting there is a problem takes courage, but it is the foundation of change. Ask yourself, "What role did I play in this situation?" and "What can I do differently next time?" Facing these questions might feel uncomfortable, but denial is far more damaging in the long run.

Without support, knowledge, and guidance, unresolved anger can destroy relationships, family bonds, career opportunities, and even your own sense of peace. But the good news is that help exists, and it works. Anger management is not just for "angry people." It is for anyone who wants to improve emotional balance and live better.

These programs are not lectures or punishments. They are full of practical tools, activities, and insights designed for everyone—children, teens, couples, and families alike. With the right awareness and techniques, anyone can transform anger from a destructive emotion into a force for personal growth and strength.

ꕥ

# 2

# RECOGNISING THE MANY FACES OF ANGER

Anger is not a single emotion. It appears in many forms, shaped by personality, upbringing, and experience. Recognising what kind of anger you experience most often helps you manage it more effectively. Each type has its own pattern, and once you understand the pattern, you can begin to respond rather than react.

**Behavioural Anger**

This is the direct, "in-your-face" kind of anger. People with behavioural anger do not hold back. They confront the source of irritation, sometimes with harsh words or even physical aggression. This anger is raw and highly visible. It can quickly escalate from frustration to outburst.

The danger lies in its impulsiveness. What feels like a momentary release can lead to regret, damaged relationships, or even legal trouble. If you ever feel your anger rising to the point where you might harm someone or yourself, step away immediately.

Pause before reacting, count to ten, breathe deeply, or leave the environment. Express your feelings once calm has returned. Physical activity, such as walking or exercising, can help diffuse the built-up tension. If violent urges occur often, professional support is essential.

**Chronic Anger**

This is the "angry all the time for no clear reason" type. People with chronic anger carry an invisible storm inside them. The irritation never really ends. It might come from years of disappointment, stress, or unresolved hurt. They fume at the world, at others, and often at themselves.

Chronic anger can lead to exhaustion, strained relationships, and health issues like high blood pressure or insomnia. It becomes a habit that rewires how you see the world.

To manage it, start identifying the recurring sources of frustration. Keep a journal to track what triggers your anger and what follows it. Introduce daily calming habits: slow breathing, quiet reflection, or time in nature. Practising gratitude, even for small things, helps shift focus from resentment to balance. If you constantly feel tense or irritable, consider seeking counselling to understand what lies beneath the anger.

**Constructive Anger**

Not all anger is harmful. When handled wisely, it becomes a force for positive change. Constructive anger drives you to take action, solve problems, or stand up for fairness. It is anger that builds rather than destroys.

Channel this energy into something meaningful. Work on improving a situation instead of attacking a person. Write down your thoughts, plan a solution, or use physical activity to direct your emotions productively. People who transform anger into motivation tend to become calmer and more resilient over time.

**Deliberate Anger**

Some people use anger as a tactic to gain control. They might pretend to be angry to intimidate or manipulate others. This deliberate anger is performative; it is more about power than emotion. Over time, it damages trust and pushes people away.

If you find yourself using anger to get your way, pause and ask what you are really afraid of losing. Manipulative anger can be a learned behaviour, often picked up in childhood, but it can be unlearned through honesty and self-reflection. Healthy relationships cannot survive on fear or control, so this pattern must be addressed early before it grows into emotional abuse.

**Judgmental Anger**

Judgmental anger hides behind superiority. It shows up as criticism, constant correction, or public humiliation of others. The person believes they are right and others are wrong, which feeds arrogance and resentment.

This type of anger often stems from insecurity or perfectionism. When you tear others down, it is often because you feel small inside. The antidote is empathy. Before reacting, take a breath and consider the other person's circumstances. Remind yourself that criticism rarely heals; understanding does.

### Overwhelming Anger

This form of anger feels all-consuming. It takes over until you can no longer think clearly. You may lash out verbally or physically because the pressure inside feels unbearable. It often occurs when emotional pain, exhaustion, or trauma has not been addressed.

This type of anger is serious. It can result in self-harm, violence, or deep regret. When you feel anger rising beyond control, step away, breathe, and find a safe space. Seek help if these episodes happen frequently. Talk to a counsellor or therapist who can guide you through coping techniques and emotional regulation. You do not have to face this alone, and waiting too long can make things worse.

### Paranoid Anger

Paranoid anger comes from suspicion and mistrust. People experiencing it often believe others are against them, even without evidence. They might misinterpret innocent comments as insults or view neutral actions as threats.

This type of anger can be isolating. It damages relationships and fuels anxiety. To manage it, slow down before reacting. Ask yourself whether there is proof of what you believe or if it might be an assumption. Talk to someone neutral to get a perspective. If you often find yourself angry about imagined situations, professional support can help rebuild trust and emotional balance.

### Passive Anger

Passive anger hides behind silence, sarcasm, and subtle criticism. Instead of confrontation, people express resentment through indirect means like cold behaviour, sarcasm, or deliberate procrastination.

This anger is often rooted in fear of conflict. It can quietly poison relationships over time because nothing is ever addressed openly. The best approach is to practise honest communication. Say how you feel clearly and calmly instead of hinting or mocking. Repressed anger is still anger; it simply leaks out in smaller, more damaging ways.

**Retaliatory Anger**

Retaliatory anger is the quick, defensive response that strikes back when provoked. Someone criticises you, and you immediately react. It is the "you hurt me, I'll hurt you" kind of emotion. While it might feel satisfying in the moment, it keeps you trapped in cycles of hostility and regret.

To manage it, pause before responding. Remind yourself that reacting instantly often worsens the situation. Not every attack requires a counterattack. Sometimes silence or walking away is the strongest form of self-control.

**Self-Inflicted Anger**

This is anger directed inward. Instead of expressing emotion outwardly, people blame or punish themselves. It often appears in those struggling with guilt, addiction, or low self-esteem. They hold themselves to impossible standards and respond to failure with self-criticism or self-harm.

This kind of anger can be dangerous if ignored. It can lead to depression or destructive behaviour. The first step to healing is self-compassion. Acknowledge that everyone makes mistakes. Replace self-blame with small acts of care. Writing down your thoughts, talking to a therapist, or sharing feelings with someone you trust can lighten the emotional load.

If your anger toward yourself ever turns into thoughts of self-harm, reach out immediately to a professional or a trusted friend. Seeking help is not a weakening act.

**Verbal Anger**

Verbal anger uses words as weapons. The shouting, insults, or cutting remarks might not leave visible scars, but they can wound deeply. People who use words this way often regret them later, but by then, the damage is done.

To manage it, pause before speaking. Count to ten or take a deep breath before you respond. Learn to express your feelings calmly instead of attacking. Apologise sincerely when you say something hurtful, and focus on improving your communication skills. Words can heal as powerfully as they can harm, so use them with care.

**Volatile Anger**

Volatile anger is quick to ignite and quick to fade. It can flare up over something minor and disappear moments later, leaving everyone else stunned. Although these outbursts may seem harmless because they pass quickly, they can create lasting fear and instability in relationships.

This kind of anger comes from poor impulse control. To manage it, work on recognising early signs such as clenched fists, rapid heartbeat, or tension in your chest. When you notice these signals, step away, breathe deeply, or distract yourself with movement until the intensity subsides. Regular mindfulness, journaling, or physical exercise can help build emotional stability.

If volatile anger leads to repeated conflict or fear in your relationships, it is important to seek guidance. Consistent emotional outbursts can be a sign of deeper stress or unresolved trauma that needs attention.

ꕥ

# 3

# UNEARTHING THE ROOTS

## Common Causes and Consequences of Anger

We don't learn anger in isolation. We pick it up from the people and environments around us. The way we express or suppress anger is often a reflection of what we saw growing up. If you were surrounded by people who shouted to be heard, sulked to gain sympathy, or bottled up their frustration, those patterns may have become part of your own emotional vocabulary.

The good news is that anything learned can be unlearned. Emotional habits can be replaced with healthier ones through awareness and consistent effort. The first step in managing anger is understanding where it comes from and how it operates inside us.

### The Science Behind Anger

Anger begins in the brain before we ever raise our voice or clench a fist. When we perceive a threat, the amygdala, the brain's emotional alarm centre, activates instantly. It sends signals that release stress hormones such as adrenaline and cortisol. These chemicals prepare the body for action—heart rate increases, muscles tense, and breathing quickens.

This "fight or flight" response evolved to protect us from danger, but in modern life, the same system can trigger over small frustrations, like traffic jams or criticism at work. When this happens repeatedly, our nervous system stays in a constant state of alert, making it easier to lose control over minor irritations. Learning to calm this biological reaction through breathing, mindfulness, or physical release helps prevent anger from hijacking your rational mind.

**Common Triggers and Root Causes**

Anger often masks deeper emotions such as fear, shame, sadness, or frustration. Understanding your triggers helps you respond thoughtfully instead of reacting impulsively. These triggers usually fall into three categories:

1. **External Triggers**

   These are events or circumstances outside your control, traffic delays, arguments, noisy environments, workplace stress, or financial pressure. When external triggers pile up, they can overwhelm your coping capacity. Recognising them early allows you to pause, take a breath, and address what you can change rather than what you cannot.

   **Healthy alternative:**

   If you often find yourself reacting to external chaos, focus on developing rituals that restore calm, such as listening to music during commutes, scheduling short breaks at work, or practising relaxation techniques at the end of stressful days.

2. **Internal Triggers**

   Internal triggers come from thoughts and beliefs that amplify anger. These include perfectionism, fear of failure, low self-esteem, or unresolved grief. When expectations are rigid or self-critical, even small setbacks can spark disproportionate reactions. For example, believing that others "should" always behave a certain way leads to disappointment and irritation when they don't.

   **Healthy alternative:**

   Challenge absolute thinking. Replace "should" and "must" with more flexible language like "I'd prefer" or "I'd like." Practising self-compassion reduces the emotional pressure that fuels anger.

3. **Social and Learned Triggers**

   Cultural norms, family patterns, and social environments strongly influence how we handle anger. In some households, expressing emotion is discouraged, while in others, loud confrontation is normal. People may also model behaviour from peers or media, believing aggression equals strength.

   **Healthy alternative:**

   Start observing what kind of anger expression feels automatic versus what feels chosen. Awareness helps you break inherited patterns and develop your own emotionally mature style of response.

### The Hidden Cost of Bottled Anger

Suppressing anger might seem like the polite or mature thing to do, but over time, it can take a serious toll on your physical and emotional health. When anger is not expressed healthily, the body remains in a state of low-grade stress. Over months or years, this can lead to high blood pressure, headaches, digestive issues, heart disease, and weakened immunity.

Emotionally, bottled-up anger often reappears as anxiety, resentment, or depression. People who suppress anger tend to withdraw, feel misunderstood, or experience a general loss of joy. Relationships suffer when unspoken frustration builds walls between people.

Unmanaged anger can also lead to more visible consequences such as domestic violence, verbal abuse, addiction, and self-destructive behaviour. The longer anger goes unaddressed, the more likely it is to harden into bitterness or hopelessness.

**Reflection Exercise:**

- When was the last time you felt anger rising but kept it to yourself?
- What physical sensations did you notice: tightness in the chest, clenched jaw, racing heart?
- What would a healthier way of expressing that emotion look like next time?

If you notice that your anger frequently causes you to lash out or withdraw, or if it disrupts your work and relationships, consider seeking professional guidance. Early help prevents anger from becoming a permanent lens through which you see the world.

**The Ripple Effect of Uncontrolled Anger**

The effects of unmanaged anger go far beyond the moment of the outburst. Physically, chronic anger keeps the body flooded with stress hormones, leading to fatigue, weakened immunity, and a higher risk of illness. Mentally, it clouds judgment and decision-making, often resulting in choices that damage one's credibility or relationships.

Professionally, repeated displays of anger can affect teamwork, promotions, and trust. Emotionally, it narrows your ability to empathise and connect, replacing curiosity with defensiveness. Over time, anger can isolate you, making the world feel like a constant battle instead of a place for growth and connection.

**Reflection Exercise:**

- Think of a recent situation where anger led to a consequence you regret. What could you have done differently?
- How does your anger affect the people you care about most?
- What would "peace" look like in your daily life if anger no longer controlled your reactions?

**Moving Toward Awareness and Change**

Managing anger does not mean suppressing it. It means learning to listen to its message without letting it take over. Every angry impulse carries information about a boundary crossed, an unmet need, or a wound unhealed. The goal is not to silence anger, but to understand what it is trying to tell you.

Start by paying attention to your emotional patterns. Note when your reactions feel stronger than the situation requires. Keep a journal of recurring triggers and how you handled them. Over time, you will start to see patterns: moments where a pause, a deep breath, or a simple change in words could have altered the outcome.

**Healthy alternative:** Replace the idea of "controlling anger" with "guiding anger." One focuses on suppression; the other focuses on direction. Guided anger can motivate change, encourage assertiveness, and strengthen self-awareness.

**The Path Forward**

Anger is not an enemy; it is an emotion that signals something important needs attention. By understanding how it works, what fuels it, and what it costs you, you begin to reclaim control. This is the foundation of emotional intelligence, the ability to respond rather than react.

Awareness turns anger from a destructive force into a teacher. With patience, practice, and support, you can transform moments of fury into opportunities for insight, empathy, and balance.

ꙮ

# 4

# THE "BAD SEED" AND PERSONAL TRIGGERS

The rise in violent behaviour and poor anger control among children and teenagers often makes people wonder if some individuals are simply born bad. It is a question that has worried parents, teachers, and psychologists for decades. Why do some young people seem to lose control more easily? Are they born with a tendency toward aggression, or is it something they learn from the world around them? The truth is that no one is born bad. Human beings are born with different temperaments, and some children are naturally more sensitive, reactive, or impulsive.

**The Role of Biology in Anger**

These biological traits may make them more likely to express anger quickly, but they do not predetermine who they will become. The environment a person grows up in, the way they are loved, taught, and disciplined, shapes how those traits unfold. Scientific studies show that stress during pregnancy can influence a baby's developing brain.

When a mother experiences chronic stress, her body releases hormones that can make the baby's nervous system more reactive to frustration later in life. Similarly, very high levels of testosterone can make some people more impulsive, while low serotonin levels can make it harder to calm down after anger. Even small injuries to the frontal lobes, the part of the brain that controls impulses, can make emotional regulation more difficult.

### The Power of Environment and Learning

But these biological influences are only one side of the story. The much larger influence comes from the environment and learning. A child who grows up around love, clear rules, and calm communication learns that emotions can be handled safely. A child raised in an atmosphere of shouting, humiliation, or neglect learns that control and dominance are the only ways to survive. Both kinds of learning become habits that continue into adulthood unless they are consciously changed.

### How We Learn Anger

People also learn about anger through imitation. When children watch adults lose their temper, insult others, or throw objects when upset, they remember those reactions. Even if the adults later apologise, the child has already learned the association between frustration and aggression. The same is true for adults who grew up in such homes. If they were surrounded by anger for years, they may find themselves reacting the same way as adults without realising why. These habits are deeply rooted, but they can be changed with awareness and effort.

Understanding where anger comes from makes it easier to control. Anger is not always triggered by big events. It can rise in simple moments—when we feel disrespected, ignored, or treated unfairly. It can also appear when we are tired, hungry, or overwhelmed. Many people notice they are more irritable after a stressful day or when something does not go as planned. These situations do not create anger on their own; they simply trigger emotions that were already building underneath.

Recognising your triggers is one of the most useful skills you can learn. Try to notice what situations make you react quickly. Do certain people, words, or tones set you off? Are there specific themes, like feeling criticised or left out, that come up repeatedly? Once you identify your triggers, you can start preparing for them. Instead of being surprised by your reaction, you can decide ahead of time how you want to respond.

**The Body's Warning Signs**

Anger also shows up physically. The heart beats faster, breathing becomes shallow, muscles tighten, and the body floods with adrenaline. These are signs that your body is preparing to act. The moment you notice these sensations, you have a small window to intervene. Take a slow breath, unclench your hands, and focus your attention on something neutral. This short pause gives your thinking brain time to return to control. It may sound simple, but this small act of awareness can stop a full-outburst before it happens.

Sometimes anger feels much stronger than the situation deserves. When this happens, it usually means the anger is connected to something older, perhaps a memory of being blamed unfairly, rejected, or humiliated. The present moment activates an older emotional wound.

By paying attention to these patterns, you can begin to separate the past from the present and react more appropriately to what is actually happening.

**Teaching Emotional Intelligence to Children**

Children experience this too. When a child lashes out, it often means they are feeling unheard, scared, or overwhelmed. Punishment alone does not solve this. What they need is understanding and guidance. Teaching them to recognise emotions, talk about what bothers them, and use calm-down techniques builds lifelong emotional intelligence. You can say things like, "It's okay to be angry, but let's figure out what to do about it." This helps them feel safe while learning self-control. Adults must also be aware of the examples they set. If a parent or caregiver handles frustration calmly, children learn by watching. They see that anger can be managed without yelling or hurting others. On the other hand, if a parent shouts or uses harsh words, children internalise that as normal. Changing your own habits might feel difficult at first, but each calm reaction becomes a lesson that your children will remember far longer than any lecture. Even adults who live alone benefit from self-awareness. If you notice that small problems set you off, look for physical or lifestyle factors that may be adding to your frustration. Lack of sleep, dehydration, hunger, and chronic stress all make patience harder. Taking care of your body is one of the simplest and most effective ways to reduce anger. A tired or undernourished body is a restless one. Regular sleep, balanced meals, and exercise give you a stronger foundation for emotional control.

When anger becomes constant or intense, it may also indicate unresolved emotional pain. Bottled-up resentment, trauma, or guilt can resurface as irritability. If you feel that your anger is controlling you rather than the other way around, it may be time to seek professional help. Therapy can help you explore the real sources of anger and teach practical techniques to respond differently. There is no shame in seeking help. In fact, it shows responsibility and a willingness to grow.

When anger crosses into violence, verbal abuse, or fear, it is no longer a private problem. It becomes a safety issue. People who live in households where anger is uncontrolled often suffer deep emotional harm that lasts for years. Getting help early protects everyone involved. If you ever feel unsafe, reach out to a counsellor, doctor, or trusted organisation that handles emotional support. Help is available, and change is always possible.

### Building New Habits of Calm

Breaking old anger patterns takes time, but every step counts. The moment you recognise a trigger and choose to stay calm, you are already building a new habit. With practice, your brain learns that anger can exist without destruction. The result is not suppression, but mastery. Over time, anger becomes less of a threat and more of a signal, a reminder that something inside you needs attention, not punishment.

Calm is learned the same way anger is learned: through repetition. Every time you pause before reacting, you are teaching yourself that peace is possible. When you do this consistently, you begin to experience a deeper kind of strength, the kind that comes from self-control, understanding, and compassion. That strength changes not only how you respond to the world, but how the world responds to you.

⁂

L E A P Learning Empowerment & Achieving Potential

# The Impact of Uncontrolled Anger

# 5

# THE SHADOW OF ANGER

## Domestic Violence and Child Abuse

Anger, when left unchecked, can turn from a personal struggle into something far more destructive. It can consume relationships, families, and homes. The most painful expression of uncontrolled anger is violence within one's own family. Domestic violence and child abuse are not just about physical harm. They are about control, fear, and emotional pain that often begins with poor anger management.

Many people imagine anger as an explosive outburst, a sudden act of rage, but in truth, it often builds quietly. A person may feel ignored, powerless, or rejected, and the resentment grows until it erupts in harmful ways. These outbursts can leave behind deep wounds that are emotional as much as physical. What makes domestic violence so painful is that it occurs between people who are supposed to care for each other.

## Understanding the Roots of Domestic Anger

Violence rarely begins overnight. It usually starts with small acts such as verbal insults, controlling behaviour, or humiliation that gradually intensify. Behind this anger is often insecurity and fear. Many individuals who resort to aggression have low self-esteem, a need to dominate, or a belief that losing control means losing respect. Others may have grown up in homes where violence was normalised, learning that anger is a way to solve problems or establish power.

In families where shouting and physical punishment were common, children internalise that aggression equals authority. As adults, they may not realise that this pattern is harmful because it feels familiar. What they once feared as children becomes the very behaviour they repeat. Without intervention, the cycle continues across generations.

Substance abuse adds another layer of risk. Alcohol or drugs lower inhibitions and distort judgment, making people more likely to lash out. Anger mixed with intoxication often leads to extreme and unpredictable behaviour. When this pattern becomes frequent, relationships can shift from loving to dangerous very quickly.

It is important to understand that anger does not cause abuse on its own. Abuse is a choice. While anger can influence emotions, violent actions are deliberate. People who use anger as a weapon often justify their behaviour by blaming others: "You made me angry," or "I wouldn't have done this if you hadn't provoked me." But anger does not excuse violence. Responsibility always lies with the person who chooses to harm.

## The Silent Victims

Domestic violence affects everyone in the home, not just the direct victim. Children who witness parents or caregivers being violent often experience intense fear and confusion. Even if they are not physically hurt, they suffer emotional damage that can last for years. Many grow up feeling unsafe, anxious, or guilty, believing they somehow caused the conflict.

Research shows that more than 80 per cent of children who die from abuse are under the age of four. These are infants and toddlers who cannot defend themselves. In many cases, these deaths result from a momentary loss of control, a parent shaking a crying baby or striking a child out of frustration. "Shaken Baby Syndrome," one of the most tragic outcomes of uncontrolled anger, leads to permanent brain injury or death.

When parents or caregivers use physical punishment out of rage, they teach children that love and violence can coexist. This confusion damages a child's sense of trust and makes it harder for them to form healthy relationships later in life. They may grow up afraid to express feelings or, conversely, may use aggression as a way to get attention or control.

Domestic violence is not limited to one gender, but statistics show that men commit the majority of violent acts. During the Vietnam War, for instance, more women were killed in their homes than men on the battlefield. These numbers highlight how serious the issue is and how urgently anger management must be addressed in every community.

## Breaking the Cycle

The first step to ending domestic violence is recognising it. Abuse can take many forms: physical harm, threats, constant criticism, isolation, or financial control. Many victims blame themselves, thinking, "Maybe I made them angry," or "They didn't mean it." But abuse is never justified. Anger is an emotion. Violence is a choice.

If you or someone you know is experiencing abuse, the most important step is to reach out for help. Speak to a trusted friend, a counsellor, or a local helpline. Doctors, teachers, and community centres can connect victims to safe spaces and professional support. No one should face abuse alone.

For those who struggle with violent outbursts, acknowledging the problem is crucial. Denial only makes things worse. Anger management therapy can help individuals learn to pause, understand their triggers, and develop alternative ways to express frustration. Counselling provides tools to rebuild empathy, learn communication skills, and recognise the signs of rising anger before it leads to harm.

It also helps to remember that true strength lies not in control or intimidation, but in restraint. The ability to remain calm under pressure is a mark of emotional maturity. Seeking therapy is not a sign of weakness. It is a sign of courage—a decision to stop the damage and begin healing.

## The Role of Society

Communities, schools, and workplaces all play a part in preventing domestic violence. Education about anger, respect, and empathy must begin early. Teaching children to talk about feelings instead of suppressing them helps prevent violence later in life. Programs that promote self-awareness, problem-solving, and communication skills have proven effective in reducing aggressive behaviour in teens and adults alike.

Employers and institutions should also provide resources for those struggling with anger or family conflict. Workshops, counselling programs, and open discussions can help normalise help-seeking behaviour. When people understand that anger can be managed and treated, they are more likely to ask for support before a crisis occurs.

Society often treats anger and violence as private matters, but they are public health issues. Every incident of abuse affects not only individuals but the emotional fabric of entire communities. Supporting victims, holding abusers accountable, and promoting healthy emotional expression are all part of the solution.

**The Journey Toward Healing**

Healing from the shadow of anger requires both inner and outer work. Victims of abuse must be given safe environments where they can rebuild trust, while those who have caused harm must be taught accountability and empathy. This process takes time, but it is possible.

For families affected by violence, therapy and support groups can help everyone understand the roots of anger and learn new ways of communicating. Many people who once believed they could never change have found peace through therapy, faith-based support, or structured anger management programs.

The goal is not to eliminate anger, but to transform it. Anger can be a powerful force for good when channelled correctly. It can motivate people to create change, protect loved ones, and seek justice. What matters is learning how to guide that energy with awareness rather than letting it take control.

Every person has the capacity to learn, to change, and to heal. It begins with a choice to stop harm, to seek help, and to use anger not as a weapon, but as a signal for growth.

ᘓᘐ

# 6

# DESTRUCTIVE DYNAMICS

**Negative Cycles, Substance Abuse, and Emotional Immaturity**

Anger, when it takes hold of a person's life, rarely exists alone. It often joins forces with other habits and emotions that make it harder to manage—substance abuse, denial, emotional immaturity, and cycles of avoidance. Together, these elements create a web that can quietly destroy peace, stability, and relationships. Learning to understand these destructive patterns is the key to breaking them and regaining control over one's emotional life.

## Understanding Destructive Cycles

Destructive cycles often begin when anger or frustration is left unresolved. Instead of dealing with the real source of discomfort, a person tries to numb it or push it away. They might drink to unwind, lash out at others, or retreat into silence. For a short while, this might feel like relief, but it only hides the problem. The anger builds again and eventually returns stronger than before.

Each time this happens, the brain becomes more used to reacting in the same way, and the behaviour turns into a habit. Some people start to rely on anger itself as an outlet. They feel powerful when angry, or they use it to avoid feeling pain, sadness, or fear. The problem is that this “relief” is temporary, and the price is high. Every outburst damages trust, weakens relationships, and leaves guilt behind.

Substance abuse makes this pattern worse. Alcohol and drugs lower self-control and cloud judgment. Someone who is already frustrated or insecure may become more aggressive or defensive under their influence. A single drink may seem harmless, but for a person struggling with anger, intoxication can become a shortcut to disaster. When the effects wear off, shame or regret often sets in, feeding the same anger that caused the problem. The result is a continuous loop: anger leads to escape, escape leads to regret, and regret fuels more anger.

Destructive cycles can also form in quieter ways. Some people do not express their anger outwardly but turn it inward. They may isolate themselves, overwork, overeat, or engage in self-criticism. These responses still belong to the same emotional cycle; they suppress rather than resolve what’s going on inside. Over time, these behaviours wear away confidence, increase stress, and make future outbursts even more likely.

Breaking such patterns begins with awareness. You cannot change what you refuse to see. Take a step back and notice how your anger unfolds. What triggers it? What do you do afterwards? What consequences follow? Mapping these connections turns chaos into something you can understand, and once understood, it can be changed.

**Emotional Immaturity and Anger**

Emotional immaturity does not mean a lack of intelligence. It means the person has not yet developed the skills needed to process emotions in healthy, responsible ways. Emotionally immature people often act on impulse. They speak or react before thinking, avoid accountability, and blame others for their frustration. Instead of recognising anger as an emotion to be managed, they use it to control situations or people.

This behaviour often starts in childhood. Some people were never taught that it's okay to feel anger without acting on it. Others were punished for expressing emotions and learned to hide them until they burst. Without guidance, these habits carry into adulthood, showing up in patterns such as passive aggression, defensiveness, or explosive temper.

Emotional maturity begins when a person learns to pause and name what they are feeling. Instead of reacting immediately, they identify the message behind the emotion. Anger often signals that something feels unfair, that a boundary has been crossed, or that a need has been ignored. Recognising that message allows for calm action instead of chaos.

A mature response might sound like, "I'm upset because I felt dismissed," rather than, "You never listen to me." The first expresses emotion and invites understanding; the second attacks and provokes. The difference lies not in what is felt, but in how it is communicated.

Developing emotional maturity takes practice. It requires honesty and humility, the willingness to admit mistakes and learn new ways of thinking. People who are used to shouting, shutting down, or avoiding conflict often find that these reactions no longer work once they begin seeking balance. They discover that calmness is not weakness; it is emotional strength in action.

**The Role of Substance Abuse in Anger**

Substance use and anger feed off each other. Anger can drive people to drink or use drugs, while those substances lower inhibitions and make anger harder to control. It becomes a partnership that damages both mental and physical health.

Alcohol, for example, slows brain activity in areas that regulate judgment and impulse control. This is why even mild intoxication can lead to reckless words or behaviour. Drugs that stimulate the nervous system, such as cocaine or methamphetamine, heighten aggression and paranoia, while depressants like opioids and sedatives can trap people in cycles of emotional numbness followed by guilt.

Breaking free requires treating both issues together. Focusing only on substance use without addressing anger will not work because the emotions that led to the habit remain unresolved. Likewise, trying to manage anger while still drinking or using substances makes emotional control almost impossible. Recovery programs and anger management therapy are most effective when combined, providing structure, accountability, and new coping tools.

For anyone struggling with both, the first step is honesty; acknowledging the full picture. Many people live in denial for years, convincing themselves they have control when they don't. Admitting the truth is uncomfortable but liberating. It marks the beginning of genuine change.

**Breaking Free from the Pattern**

Ending a destructive cycle takes more than willpower. It requires awareness, support, and consistent practice. Begin by paying attention to what happens right before you react. What thoughts go through your mind? What physical sensations do you notice? These are signals that your emotions are rising. Learning to recognise them early gives you a chance to interrupt the pattern before it takes over.

Once you are aware, create replacement habits. When you feel anger building, step away, take a deep breath, or focus on a simple grounding task such as counting or stretching. Over time, these actions train your body to pause instead of exploding.

Keeping a journal can also help. Writing down what happened, what you felt, and how you responded gives clarity. Patterns that once seemed invisible become easier to identify. You may begin to notice that the same few situations or emotions trigger most of your reactions. Understanding this is empowering; it gives you a choice where before there was only habit.

Support is another key part of recovery. Surround yourself with people who encourage accountability. Join groups or talk to counsellors who understand anger and addiction. When you feel supported, it becomes easier to stay consistent. Progress may be slow, but consistency will transform even the most ingrained habits.

**Rebuilding Emotional Strength**

Emotional maturity grows with self-awareness. The more you understand what drives your emotions, the less they control you. Begin by shifting your language. Instead of saying, "They made me angry," try saying, "I felt angry when that happened." This small change helps you take ownership of your reactions. Responsibility builds strength, while blame keeps you trapped.

Repairing relationships is also part of rebuilding emotional maturity. Anger often leaves behind guilt, distance, or misunderstanding. Reaching out to apologise, communicate, and make amends helps heal both sides. True maturity means caring enough to fix what anger has broken, even when it feels difficult.

Finally, remember that peace is a practice. It is not achieved in a single day but through repeated effort. Every calm response, every choice to walk away or breathe instead of shout, becomes a brick in the foundation of emotional balance. Over time, this new way of responding becomes second nature, replacing chaos with clarity and tension with peace.

ജ൬

7

# EXTREME REACTIONS

**Trauma Responses and Intermittent Explosive Disorder**

Most people experience anger as a passing emotion, something that rises and fades with time. But for some, anger feels uncontrollable, explosive, and far out of proportion to the situation. It can appear suddenly, with a level of intensity that surprises even the person experiencing it. When anger begins to take on a life of its own, it may be a sign that something deeper is happening beneath the surface.

Anger at this level often connects to unresolved trauma or underlying psychological conditions. These are not signs of weakness or moral failure. They are emotional injuries that need care and healing. Understanding how trauma affects the brain and body helps explain why some people seem to live in a constant state of alertness or rage, even when nothing dangerous is happening around them.

**Anger as a Response to Trauma**

Trauma can come from many sources: childhood neglect, abuse, accidents, violence, or loss. It leaves a lasting mark on both the mind and the body. When a person experiences trauma, the brain's alarm system becomes highly sensitive. It learns to expect danger and reacts instantly, even to harmless triggers. This means that anger can surface not because of the present moment, but because the body is remembering a past threat.

In people who have experienced trauma, the nervous system often stays on high alert. Their bodies may produce stress hormones more frequently, keeping them tense and restless. A raised voice, a closed door, or even a certain expression on someone's face can make them feel threatened, leading to an intense reaction. This is why trauma survivors sometimes feel anger "out of nowhere." Their bodies are not responding to today; they are reacting to yesterday's fear.

This type of anger is often protective. It is a shield that the mind builds to prevent further hurt. Unfortunately, it can also damage relationships and self-esteem. People who react in anger may later feel guilty or confused, not understanding why they couldn't stay calm. Recognising this as a trauma response, not a personality flaw, is the first step toward healing.

Therapies that focus on trauma can help. Approaches such as trauma-focused cognitive behavioural therapy (CBT), somatic therapy, or Eye Movement Desensitisation and Reprocessing (EMDR) allow the body and brain to process painful experiences safely. Over time, these methods reduce the sense of constant threat and make emotional control easier. Healing trauma requires patience, compassion, and professional guidance, but it is possible.

## When Anger Becomes a Disorder

For some people, anger appears as sudden bursts of aggression that seem impossible to predict or control. These individuals may suffer from a condition called Intermittent Explosive Disorder (IED). It is a recognised mental health disorder characterised by repeated episodes of intense anger or violent behaviour that are far greater than the situation calls for.

A person with IED might scream, break things, or even become physically aggressive over a minor irritation. Afterwards, they often feel remorse, shame, or exhaustion. These episodes can last only minutes but leave emotional and physical consequences that linger for days. Unlike ordinary frustration, IED is not about choice. It involves neurological and chemical imbalances that make it hard for the brain to regulate emotion and impulse.

The causes of IED are still being studied, but they are believed to include genetic factors, brain chemistry, and early exposure to violence or neglect. It often begins during adolescence and can continue into adulthood if untreated. The good news is that professional treatment can make a major difference. A combination of therapy and, in some cases, medication helps stabilise mood and improve impulse control. Cognitive-behavioural therapy teaches individuals to identify warning signs, challenge distorted thoughts, and practise calming techniques before anger takes over.

If you or someone you know has outbursts that feel uncontrollable, it is important to seek professional help. With the right support, it is entirely possible to regain control and build a calmer, more balanced life.

## Healing and Rebuilding Safety

People dealing with trauma-related anger or IED often live in a state of fear, the fear of their own reactions. This fear can make them withdraw from others, avoid confrontation, or suppress emotions completely. But avoiding emotion only increases pressure. Healing begins by creating a sense of safety, both physically and emotionally.

Simple grounding techniques can help restore a feeling of calm. These might include focusing on slow, steady breathing, naming objects in the room, or feeling your feet on the ground. Such exercises remind the body that it is no longer in danger. Over time, they retrain the nervous system to recognise the difference between past and present.

Establishing predictable routines also supports emotional balance. Regular sleep, healthy meals, and physical activity help regulate mood. Mindfulness practices, like gentle yoga or meditation, can teach awareness of early signs of anger, giving space to respond rather than react.

Rebuilding trust is another part of recovery. Trauma and extreme anger can strain relationships, but communication and vulnerability help repair them. Sharing fears, apologising for hurtful reactions, and explaining the process of healing allow others to understand what you are going through. Most importantly, it reminds you that you are not alone.

If trauma or explosive anger has made you feel hopeless, remember that change is possible. The brain and body are designed to adapt and heal. Each act of awareness—each decision to pause, breathe, and seek help—creates a new pathway toward peace.

ꕥ

L E A P Learning Empowerment & Achieving Potential

# Building Emotional Control

# 8

# FOUNDATIONAL SKILLS

**Learning to Manage Your Anger Efficiently**

Understanding anger is only half the journey. The next step is learning how to manage it before it manages you. Anger itself is not the enemy. It becomes harmful only when it takes control of your decisions and behaviour. Managing anger efficiently means recognising it early, responding thoughtfully, and developing habits that prevent it from growing into something destructive.

Learning these skills is not about suppressing emotions or pretending to be calm when you are not. It is about balance. When you learn how to express anger in healthy ways, it stops being a force of destruction and becomes a tool for understanding, communication, and change.

## Recognising Early Warning Signs

Every emotion starts with a signal. Anger often arrives with physical sensations before thoughts even form. Your body begins to tense. Your heart rate increases. Your jaw tightens, and your breathing becomes shallow. These are early signs that your body is preparing for confrontation.

When you notice these sensations, you have a small but powerful window of opportunity. This is the moment to pause and take control. Many people miss this stage and only realise they are angry once they are already yelling or reacting. Training yourself to recognise the first signs helps prevent that.

Start by paying attention to patterns. Notice what situations, people, or thoughts cause these sensations. Keep track of them in a journal or a simple list on your phone. The more aware you become of your body's cues, the earlier you can intervene.

**The Power of Pausing**

Pausing is one of the simplest yet most powerful anger management tools. When you feel your temper rising, step back—physically, mentally, or emotionally. Take a breath. If possible, walk away from the situation for a few minutes. This gives your brain time to move from emotional reaction to rational thought.

Even a short pause helps prevent words or actions that might cause regret later. It allows you to think clearly, assess the situation, and decide how you want to respond instead of reacting automatically. Over time, this pause becomes a habit, turning what once felt uncontrollable into something you can manage calmly.

If stepping away is not possible, try silent breathing. Slowly inhale through your nose for four counts, hold for two, and exhale through your mouth for six. This slows the body's fight-or-flight response and signals to your mind that it is safe to relax.

**Using Perspective to Calm the Mind**

Anger narrows your thinking. It convinces you that the situation is urgent and that you must react immediately. But most conflicts are not as urgent as they feel. By stepping back mentally, you can see the bigger picture. Ask yourself, "Will this matter in a week? In a month? In a year?" This simple question helps restore perspective.

You can also try reinterpreting the situation. Maybe the driver who cut you off is late for work. Maybe your colleague's tone was rude because they are stressed, not because they wanted to insult you. Perspective does not excuse poor behaviour, but it helps you understand it differently, which reduces emotional intensity.

**Communication: Expressing Anger Constructively**

Anger often becomes destructive when it is bottled up or expressed aggressively. Constructive expression means communicating what you feel without attacking, blaming, or humiliating others. Instead of saying, "You never listen to me," try, "I feel frustrated when I don't feel heard." This keeps the focus on your feelings, not the other person's faults.

Timing also matters. Speaking when emotions are still high rarely helps. Wait until you have calmed down, then address the issue clearly. If the conversation feels too heated, suggest returning to it later. Managing tone and timing allows discussions to solve problems rather than create new ones.

When others express anger toward you, try to listen without taking it personally. Sometimes people simply need to feel heard. By staying calm, you give them space to release frustration without escalating the situation. Responding calmly does not mean agreeing; it means refusing to add more fuel to the fire.

### Releasing Physical Tension

Because anger triggers a physical response, it must be released physically as well. Holding anger in the body causes stress, tightness, and fatigue. Find safe, healthy outlets to release that energy. Physical activity is one of the best tools for managing anger.

Go for a walk, run, swim, or engage in any activity that raises your heart rate. Exercise helps the body burn off excess adrenaline and promotes the release of endorphins. They are natural chemicals that improve mood. Even five to ten minutes of brisk movement can make a difference.

Creative activities such as drawing, writing, playing an instrument, or gardening can also channel frustration into expression. The goal is not to ignore the emotion but to give it a healthy direction.

### Building Emotional Resilience

Emotional resilience is the ability to stay calm and steady under pressure. It is what allows people to recover quickly from stress instead of being consumed by it. Building resilience takes time and daily practice.

Start by taking care of your body and mind. Regular sleep, balanced nutrition, and moments of relaxation strengthen your emotional stability. When you are tired or run down, patience becomes harder to maintain.

Practising mindfulness also builds resilience. Mindfulness means being aware of your emotions without judging them. When you feel anger rising, acknowledge it silently: "I am feeling angry right now." Simply naming the emotion creates distance between you and the feeling. This distance gives you room to choose your response.

**The Role of Reflection and Self-Awareness**

Reflection turns experience into growth. After an anger episode, take a few minutes to think about what happened. What triggered you? What did you feel before and after? Did you handle it well, or is there something you would change next time?

Writing down your reflections helps solidify learning. You begin to recognise patterns, strengths, and areas for improvement. Over time, this kind of awareness transforms your relationship with anger. It becomes less of an enemy and more of a teacher.

Anger can reveal important truths about what matters to you. It can show you when your values are being challenged or when your boundaries are being crossed. The goal is to understand the message behind the emotion and address it calmly, rather than letting the emotion dictate your actions.

ജ്ഞ

# 9

# HEALTHY STRATEGIES AND THREE CORE APPROACHES TO ANGER

Anger management is not about ignoring or suppressing emotion. It is about recognising that anger is energy, powerful, and potentially destructive, and learning how to guide it in a healthy direction. When handled correctly, this same energy can become motivation, focus, and assertiveness. When left uncontrolled, it becomes rage, resentment, and harm.

There are many proven methods used by therapists and counsellors around the world to help people manage anger. These techniques aim to help individuals with short tempers control their reactions and channel frustration into positive outlets rather than destructive ones. Outbursts of rage, violent behaviour, or negative responses to stress are often signs that a person is struggling to cope with underlying emotions. Help should always be sought before anger turns reckless or violent.

At the heart of every anger management strategy lies one simple idea: you must understand what triggers your anger before you can control it. Anger is rarely about a single event. It often reflects deeper emotions like fear, hurt, frustration, or feeling disrespected. The goal of anger management is to help people recognise these underlying emotions and respond in ways that are acceptable, constructive, and emotionally safe.

**Recognising the Need for Help**

The first and most important step is to acknowledge that uncontrolled anger is a problem. Many people avoid seeking help because they believe anger is natural or justified. While anger itself is normal, repeated outbursts or violent reactions indicate an underlying issue that needs attention. Recognising the problem is not a sign of weakness. It is an act of responsibility.

Counsellors often begin by helping individuals take ownership of their emotions and behaviour. You cannot control what others do, but you can control your response. Reflecting on past incidents—what triggered your anger, how you reacted, and what the outcome was- helps reveal patterns that can be changed.

Understanding that anger often hides other emotions such as sadness, jealousy, or guilt is essential. Identifying these emotions helps prevent confusion and gives you a clearer idea of what you truly need in that moment: comfort, respect, understanding, or rest.

**The Three Core Approaches to Managing Anger**

There are three primary ways people handle anger. These are known as suppressing, expressing, and calming. Every effective anger management plan draws from one or more of these approaches.

1. **Suppressing Anger**

   Suppressing does not mean denying that anger exists. It means learning to control the initial reaction and redirecting the energy toward something productive. People who tend to react impulsively often find this method helpful because it gives them a pause between emotion and action.

   Redirecting anger can take many forms: exercising, writing, cleaning, or doing any activity that absorbs focus and releases physical energy. The goal is to prevent harmful outbursts and give yourself time to think clearly before responding. Over time, suppression should lead to reflection, not repression. It works best when combined with self-awareness and calm analysis of what caused the anger in the first place.

2. **Expressing Anger**

   Expressing anger means communicating feelings in a clear, respectful, and non-violent way. The key is honesty without aggression. Many people struggle to express anger because they fear rejection or loss of control, yet healthy expression is the best way to prevent long-term resentment.

   For example, instead of shouting, "You always ignore me," a better expression would be, "I felt unheard when my opinion wasn't considered." The focus shifts from blame to emotion, making it easier for others to understand and respond. Expressing anger in this way builds stronger relationships because it replaces hostility with honesty.

3. **Calming Anger**

   Calming means addressing anger internally by regulating both the emotional and physical reactions that come with it. This involves slowing your heartbeat, relaxing muscles, and quieting thoughts before they spiral out of control. Techniques include deep breathing, counting to ten, visualising peaceful images, and repeating calming phrases such as "I am in control" or "This will pass."

Relaxing your body first helps calm your mind. Roll your shoulders, unclench your jaw, and take deep breaths from your diaphragm. Imagine yourself in a peaceful place, or recall a comforting experience. These small physical actions tell your body that the threat has passed, helping anger fade naturally.

These three core approaches: suppressing, expressing, and calming, are the foundation for most anger management techniques used in therapy and everyday life.

**Proven Strategies for Everyday Control**

The simplest anger management strategy is to remove yourself from a situation that tempts you to act impulsively. Taking a break or practising a short "time-out" allows space for emotions to settle. Go for a walk, listen to music, or sit quietly for a few minutes before re-engaging. This short pause often prevents regretful decisions.

Engaging in physical activity is another proven way to release tension. Exercise helps burn off the adrenaline and cortisol that rise when you are angry. Activities like swimming, yoga, cycling, or even cleaning can clear the mind and restore balance.

Creative outlets such as painting, writing, or playing music also help redirect emotional energy. They offer an opportunity to process feelings in a constructive, non-verbal way.

Equally effective is reflection. After an outburst or difficult day, take time to think about what happened and how you reacted. What could you do differently next time? This kind of reflection builds awareness and helps you anticipate and avoid triggers in the future.

Counsellors often recommend confronting difficult situations only after calm has been restored. Facing the source of anger while still emotional rarely leads to understanding. Once you are calm, examine the situation logically. Ask what exactly made you angry and whether it can be resolved through conversation, compromise, or acceptance. Sometimes, what once seemed infuriating turns out to be a misunderstanding.

### Additional Healthy Anger Management Techniques

Healthy anger management involves both short-term tools and long-term lifestyle changes. The following strategies can help create immediate calm while building emotional stability over time.

### Changing the Ambience

The environment plays a major role in mood and stress. Being surrounded by constant pressure, whether at home, school, or work, can build irritation. Changing your surroundings, even briefly, can refresh your mind. Take short breaks, step outside, or spend time in nature. If that's not possible, create a calm space in your home or workplace where you can unwind. Even small adjustments like soft lighting, music, or a few minutes of quiet can help reset your mood.

### Using Humour to Diffuse Tension

Humour is a powerful and often underestimated anger management tool. Laughing releases tension, shifts perspective, and prevents situations from feeling overwhelming. It is not about mocking others or avoiding issues, but about lightening the emotional load. Watching a funny show, reading something amusing, or simply smiling intentionally can change the body's chemistry and make anger easier to manage.

**Changing Your Thoughts**

How you think affects how you feel. Anger grows when thoughts become rigid or negative, such as "This always happens to me," or "People never respect me." Replacing such thoughts with more balanced ones changes your emotional response. Try reframing: instead of "They ruined my day," think, "This situation is unpleasant, but I can still stay calm." Over time, this mental shift retrains your brain to choose peace over chaos.

**Acceptance and Contemplation**

Acceptance does not mean giving up or approving of wrong behaviour. It means recognising what you can and cannot control. When you accept reality rather than resist it, frustration loses its power. Contemplation, or calmly observing your thoughts, is part of this process. Ask yourself: "What can I do to change this? What must I accept as it is?" This kind of reflection builds maturity and inner peace.

**Seeking Support and Learning More**

Learning about anger management from books, workshops, or online resources is another positive step. Education increases understanding and encourages consistent practice. For persistent or severe anger, professional guidance is invaluable. Counsellors can teach structured techniques and tailor strategies to your personality and experiences.

# 10

# PRACTICAL TECHNIQUES FOR IMMEDIATE CALM AND LONG-TERM CONTROL

Learning to manage anger effectively is a lifelong skill, not a one-time effort. It requires awareness, practice, and patience. While understanding anger's roots is essential, real change comes from applying practical techniques every day. These techniques teach both immediate calm and long-term control, helping you manage difficult emotions before they escalate into regretful actions.

**Admission and Acknowledgement of Anger**

The first and most important step in controlling anger is to admit that it exists. Many people deny their anger because they fear criticism, embarrassment, or loss of control. Others are so overwhelmed that they cannot even recognise their emotional state. But denial prevents growth. Acknowledging that anger is present allows you to take responsibility and begin managing it consciously.

Admitting anger does not mean weakness. It means self-awareness. Once you can say, "I'm angry," you create the possibility of choice, like what to do next, how to respond, and how to prevent harm. This single act of honesty transforms anger from an uncontrollable reaction into an emotion you can work with.

**Detecting the Cause of Your Anger**

After recognising anger, the next step is to understand its cause. Without clarity, you may keep reacting to symptoms rather than the real problem. Ask yourself: What triggered my anger? Was it a specific person, a memory, a fear, or an unmet expectation? Often, anger masks deeper emotions such as disappointment, insecurity, or exhaustion.

Identifying these triggers allows you to address them directly. You may realise that certain conversations, environments, or people repeatedly bring out anger. Once you know this, you can plan how to manage or avoid them. Awareness reduces surprise and increases control.

**Learning to Let Go**

One of the hardest but most liberating techniques is learning to let go of past hurts. Many people who struggle with anger replay painful events over and over, reliving resentment from the past. This keeps old emotions alive and makes present situations feel heavier than they are.

Letting go begins with forgiveness. Forgive those who have wronged you and forgive yourself for moments when you lost control. Carrying anger into the future only gives power to the past. Freeing yourself from resentment creates emotional space for peace and stability.

**Tackling Problems Instead of Fixating on Solutions**

There is a common belief that every problem has a solution. In reality, some situations cannot be "fixed" immediately, and trying too hard to find an answer can create more frustration. The key is to focus on tackling the issue rather than forcing a resolution.

For example, if a relationship or job situation cannot change right away, concentrate on how you respond to it. Adjust your expectations, set boundaries, or find coping mechanisms that reduce tension. By managing your reaction rather than obsessing over the outcome, you regain a sense of control.

**Redirecting Anger into Positive Action**

Anger carries energy, and that energy can be transformed. When you feel tension building, redirect that intensity into something constructive, exercise, cleaning, creative work, or any task that uses both body and mind. Physical activity releases stress hormones and replaces them with endorphins that promote calm and clarity.

Remember that when people are angry, they often appear stronger than they are. The real strength lies in control, not aggression. Redirecting anger into meaningful activity turns potential destruction into productivity.

**Communicating Effectively**

Anger often destroys communication, but effective communication can destroy anger. When emotions are high, you may lose awareness of your tone, words, or actions. Learning to speak calmly, listen actively, and express feelings clearly is one of the most powerful anger management tools.

Before responding in a heated conversation, take a moment to breathe and organise your thoughts. Use "I" statements to describe feelings rather than blame. For example, say, "I felt hurt when that happened," instead of "You always do this." Listening with patience and responding with care reduces defensiveness and invites understanding.

If someone else is angry, try to remain calm. Lowering your voice and speaking gently often helps the other person calm down, too. The goal is not to win an argument but to preserve respect and resolve the issue.

### Choosing to Ease Up

Easing up is a conscious decision. Anger narrows focus, making every problem seem larger than it is. Taking a step back, loosening your body, and consciously relaxing can break that intensity. Roll your shoulders, unclench your fists, and breathe deeply.

Remind yourself that anger is temporary, but the damage it causes can last. Thinking about the consequences of angry actions often helps stop them before they begin. When you ease up, you give yourself a chance to act wisely instead of reacting impulsively.

### Relaxation and Calming Exercises

Relaxation is one of the most effective and scientifically supported anger management techniques. Deep breathing exercises, meditation, or gentle yoga help slow the body's physical stress response. Mental imagery, imagining peaceful scenes or recalling positive experiences, creates calm even in the middle of chaos.

A simple exercise is to sit comfortably, close your eyes, and breathe deeply from your diaphragm. Imagine each breath washing away tension. Repeat calming phrases such as "I am safe," or "I can handle this." Over time, this practice conditions your mind to return to calm more quickly when faced with stress.

**Problem-Solving as a Long-Term Technique**

Anger often signals that something feels unfair or unresolved. Instead of reacting, focus on understanding the problem. Write it down, list the possible causes, and consider realistic solutions. You may not find an answer immediately, but thoughtful problem-solving prevents helplessness and keeps emotions from spiralling.

Staying committed to this approach develops patience. When you see yourself making progress, no matter how small, you begin to trust your ability to handle difficult emotions without losing control.

**Improving Communication Skills**

Poor communication fuels misunderstanding, and misunderstanding fuels anger. People with anger issues often react before they fully hear what others are saying. Slowing down, listening actively, and clarifying what you heard before responding helps avoid unnecessary conflict.

Practise thinking before speaking. Ask questions if something feels unclear. This not only prevents miscommunication but also shows respect, which reduces tension in conversations.

If you are in a leadership or supervisory role, maintain composure even under provocation. Communicate feedback calmly and directly. Anger may feel powerful in the moment, but calm authority earns more respect and leads to better results.

**Dealing with Everyday Provocations**

Life is unpredictable. You will meet people who frustrate or provoke you, intentionally or not. The key to peace is not avoiding anger altogether but learning how to handle it wisely. When someone deliberately tries to upset you, the best response is no reaction. Your calmness denies them the control they seek.

When irritation comes from misunderstanding, choose dialogue instead of hostility. A simple, honest conversation can dissolve resentment before it grows. Remember that anger is contagious, but so is calmness. Responding with patience can transform a tense moment into one of understanding.

**Finding Personal Outlets**

Sometimes, expressing anger directly is not appropriate, such as in formal settings or professional situations. In such cases, venting in private and harmless ways can help. Writing in a journal is one of the most effective methods. Putting thoughts on paper provides clarity and releases pressure without confrontation.

Physical outlets such as walking, running, or playing sports work in the same way. Music, art, or hobbies can also serve as release points. The key is to find a method that lets you express emotion safely and resets your perspective.

If you have made a mistake or hurt someone in anger, acknowledge it and apologise. Admitting fault is a sign of maturity and emotional intelligence, not weakness. It helps rebuild trust and prevents guilt from turning into more frustration later.

**Support and Reflection**

Support from others is vital. Confiding in a trusted friend, family member, or counsellor can provide relief and insight. Talking through emotions with someone calm and understanding helps you see situations from new angles.

Reflection and self-evaluation are equally important. Think about what triggered your anger and what helped you calm down. Use that knowledge to prepare for similar situations in the future. Every episode of anger can become a lesson in emotional growth.

**Creating a Sustainable Practice**

Managing anger is not about avoiding emotion but about maintaining balance. Incorporate calming habits into daily life—spend time in nature, practise gratitude, and stay physically active. Meditation, prayer, or silent reflection can bring spiritual peace and help you process emotions in a deeper way.

The goal is long-term stability. Over time, these practices build a foundation of calm that makes it harder for anger to take over. You will still experience irritation or frustration, but you will recover faster and respond more thoughtfully.

ℵ

# 11

# GUIDING YOUNG VOLCANOES

## Anger Management in Children and Teenagers

Children and teenagers experience anger just like adults do, but their ability to understand and control it is still developing. Each child reacts differently when frustrated or hurt. One might withdraw into silence, another might cry, while some might throw tantrums or break things. These differences can make managing anger in children feel challenging, but the key is patience and empathy.

The first step for parents, teachers, and caregivers is to recognise that every child's anger looks different. What works for one child may not work for another. Managing these reactions begins with understanding, not judgment. The goal is to help children learn how to identify what they are feeling and to express those feelings safely.

### Helping Children Build Awareness

When young children show signs of aggression, such as rolling on the ground, yelling, or throwing objects, it is important not to label them as "bad" but to help them recognise their behaviour. Awareness is the first step toward control. A child who can say, "I'm angry," or "I feel upset," is already beginning to manage their emotions.

However, anger management for children cannot follow the same approach used for adults. Younger children often lack the words to describe what they feel. Simply asking them to "talk about it" may not work. Instead, adults must use creativity to teach emotional awareness through engaging and playful methods.

Fun-based strategies, such as storytelling, role-play, drawing, and games, are especially effective. They keep children interested while teaching valuable lessons about emotions and choices. For example, colouring sheets that illustrate angry and calm behaviour, puzzles that involve resolving conflicts, or short quizzes about feelings can help children understand the consequences of their actions in a non-threatening way.

**The Playful Path to Emotional Learning**

Play is how children make sense of the world. Using play-based techniques for anger management allows them to learn without fear or pressure. When children act out scenarios through play, such as sharing toys, waiting their turn, or apologising, they develop empathy and self-control naturally.

Group games that focus on teamwork also teach patience and communication. Activities like "Feelings Charades," where kids act out emotions for others to guess, can help them recognise anger and other emotions in themselves and others. The more they understand emotions, the better they can manage them.

Play therapy and expressive arts also serve as tools for counsellors and teachers. These approaches encourage children to communicate feelings they cannot yet express verbally. Through drawing, building, or storytelling, children begin to release anger safely and understand that emotions can be managed rather than feared.

**Supporting Teenagers Through Emotional Turbulence**

Adolescence brings new challenges. Teenagers experience rapid physical, emotional, and social changes. Hormonal shifts, peer pressure, academic stress, and the desire for independence can all make anger more intense. While children may act out openly, teens often mask their emotions with silence, sarcasm, or defiance.

For parents, guiding teenagers through anger means balancing firmness with understanding. Teens need to know that anger is normal, but aggression and disrespect are not acceptable. Encouraging open dialogue helps them feel heard, which in turn reduces frustration. When a teen learns to pause, reflect, and choose their response, they begin to develop emotional maturity.

One effective way to help teenagers manage anger is to teach self-awareness. They can be encouraged to recognise the physical signs of anger—tight fists, racing heart, or flushed face—and use coping strategies before they lose control. Techniques like deep breathing, journaling, or listening to calming music can help them cool down and think clearly before reacting.

Teens should also be guided toward understanding consequences. Discussing real examples, such as losing trust, damaging relationships, or facing disciplinary actions, helps them see that uncontrolled anger has long-term effects. This reflection fosters accountability and emotional growth.

### Family Influence and the Power of Example

Children learn by observing. The way adults handle frustration becomes the model they follow. If a parent reacts to stress with shouting or aggression, children begin to see that as normal. Conversely, when adults remain calm, admit mistakes, and apologise when wrong, they teach emotional intelligence by example.

Families play a central role in helping children and teens build healthy anger management habits. Setting clear boundaries, maintaining open communication, and creating a safe emotional space at home all make a difference. Encourage family discussions where everyone can express feelings respectfully. Acknowledging a child's anger without judgment helps them feel validated, reducing the need for outbursts.

Parents and caregivers should also be aware of the external influences that affect children's emotions. Exposure to violence in media, video games, or social environments can normalise aggression. Limiting such influences and replacing them with positive experiences like sports, art, reading, and community involvement builds emotional resilience.

### Addressing Underlying Causes

Anger in children and teens is often a surface emotion. Beneath it might be fear, disappointment, loneliness, or a need for attention. Academic pressure, bullying, family conflict, or feelings of exclusion can trigger frustration. Helping children talk about these deeper issues reduces their intensity.

Professional support may be needed if anger becomes frequent, severe, or physically harmful. Counsellors and psychologists who specialise in child and adolescent behaviour can help children learn to manage emotions in a structured, safe way. Therapy programs for kids often combine fun activities, reflection, and guided discussions to help them process feelings at their own pace.

**Creative Tools and Techniques**

For younger children, tools such as worksheets, colouring pages, or picture books that show different ways to handle frustration can work wonders. Visual learning helps them remember what they see. Teaching simple breathing exercises or short "quiet time" rituals gives them immediate tools to calm down.

For teenagers, more mature activities such as journaling, exercise, art, or music provide emotional release. Writing about what they feel can help them uncover patterns in their anger and discover healthy ways to manage it. Group discussions and workshops for teens also provide a sense of belonging, reminding them that they are not alone in their struggles.

In both age groups, the focus should be on empowerment. The goal is not to suppress emotions but to teach young people that they have control over their reactions. With guidance, support, and consistent practice, children and teens learn that anger can be managed, expressed, and even transformed into motivation and empathy.

ཐ༄

LEAP Learning Empowerment & Achieving Potential

# GUIDANCE, SUPPORT, AND GROWTH

# 12

# ANGER AND COMMUNICATION

## The Power of Words

Anger does not only appear as shouting or physical outbursts. It often hides in the way we speak, the tone we use, or the silence we choose. Words can wound just as deeply as actions. A harsh remark, a sarcastic reply, or a deliberate silence can communicate anger even when we say nothing directly. The way we communicate when angry often determines whether a situation escalates or finds resolution.

When anger takes over, it affects how our brain processes information. The part of the brain responsible for emotional reactions becomes dominant, and our ability to listen and think clearly weakens. In these moments, the urge to win the argument replaces the intention to understand. We interrupt, exaggerate, and say things we later regret. This is why learning to communicate during anger is one of the most important steps in emotional growth.

Good communication does not mean avoiding anger altogether. It means expressing anger in ways that are constructive rather than destructive. Healthy communication transforms anger from something that divides people into something that reveals what truly matters. When anger is expressed with honesty and care, it can lead to greater understanding and a deeper connection.

The first tool for better communication during anger is the simple act of pausing. When you feel tension rising, stop for a moment. Breathe deeply, count slowly, or take a short walk. This pause gives your mind a chance to cool before your words create harm. Even a few seconds of stillness can prevent hours of regret.

Once calm, focus on expressing yourself clearly and respectfully. Replace blame with honesty. Instead of saying, "You always ignore me," try, "I feel hurt when I am not heard." The first statement attacks, while the second invites understanding. Using "I" statements shows ownership of your feelings rather than assigning fault. This small shift in phrasing can completely change how the other person receives your message.

The tone of voice carries as much meaning as words. A calm voice can diffuse tension, while a sharp or mocking tone can inflame it. Be mindful of your tone, facial expressions, and body language. Sometimes the words are polite, but the body communicates contempt. Align your words with your intention, so the person listening can feel your sincerity.

Timing is another powerful factor. Trying to resolve a conflict in the middle of anger rarely works. Choose the right moment to speak, when both sides are calmer and open to listening. It is better to say, "Let's talk about this later," than to force a conversation when tempers are high.

Listening is at the heart of healthy communication. Many people believe they are good listeners, but in truth, they are waiting for their turn to speak. Real listening means quieting your internal dialogue and focusing on what the other person is trying to say. It means hearing not only the words but the emotions behind them. When someone feels genuinely heard, their anger softens. Listening turns confrontation into connection.

In families, poor communication is often the root of ongoing anger. Parents may raise their voices out of frustration, and children may shut down or rebel in response. Partners may misinterpret silence as indifference or criticism as rejection. Over time, these miscommunications build resentment. Improving communication at home requires patience, empathy, and a willingness to understand before being understood. Making small efforts, such as expressing appreciation, asking questions, or acknowledging the other person's feelings, can repair years of emotional distance.

At work, communication under pressure can be equally challenging. Tight deadlines, conflicting opinions, and differing temperaments can easily spark frustration. Professional environments benefit greatly from calm, assertive communicators who can handle disagreement without hostility. When team members feel respected and heard, collaboration thrives. Leaders who model respectful communication create workplaces where anger rarely festers into conflict.

There are moments when anger becomes too intense for words to be productive. If a discussion turns hurtful or verbally abusive, the best form of communication is silence followed by space. Stepping away from an argument does not mean surrendering; it means protecting yourself and preserving the relationship. Once calm, you can revisit the issue with greater clarity and compassion.

Practising good communication during anger takes time. It requires awareness of how you speak, how you listen, and how your words affect others. Reflecting on past arguments can help. Ask yourself: What was I really trying to say? Did my words reflect my true feelings or just my frustration? How could I have expressed myself more calmly? Reflection turns every argument into a lesson in emotional intelligence.

When you learn to communicate through anger, you begin to transform relationships. Words that once hurt can now heal. Listening replaces accusation. Understanding replaces judgment. Communication becomes not just a way to express anger, but a way to transform it into empathy, growth, and connection.

### Anger in the Workplace

Work often brings out sides of us we did not know existed. It can be a place of purpose and pride, but it can also stir frustration, resentment, and anger. Deadlines, expectations, and the constant demand to perform create pressure that tests patience and emotional control. In such an environment, anger can appear in subtle ways—through irritability, harsh feedback, or withdrawal. Sometimes it shows up in quiet resistance, when you feel unappreciated or unheard despite your effort.

Anger at work is not always wrong. It can signal when boundaries are being crossed or when something important is being ignored. The problem arises when that anger turns reactive instead of reflective.

Snapping at colleagues, sending an impulsive message, or carrying bitterness into meetings may feel satisfying for a moment, but it weakens credibility and trust. The ability to pause, observe the emotion, and then choose a response is what separates emotional maturity from reactivity.

Many professionals mistake calmness for weakness. In truth, composure under stress is one of the strongest forms of authority. It commands respect without demanding it. When you can stay measured while others lose control, you influence outcomes instead of being controlled by them. This is especially true for leaders, whose tone often sets the culture of an entire team. A single outburst from a manager can undo months of motivation, while a calm, firm response can restore balance and direction.

It helps to recognise what fuels your anger at work. Is it injustice, lack of clarity, or unmet expectations? Anger often hides behind exhaustion or fear—fear of being overlooked, replaced, or misunderstood. By naming the real cause, you can decide what needs to change: the situation, your mindset, or your limits. Sometimes, the healthiest choice is not to fight harder, but to step back, reset, and return with perspective.

Practical steps make a difference. Take short breaks before reacting to stressful messages. Keep communication clear and factual, especially when emotions rise. Avoid long debates in moments of tension. When necessary, write your feelings privately first, not in an email. When you do speak, aim to solve rather than prove.

Anger, when managed wisely, becomes a source of drive. It can push you to correct unfairness, improve systems, or assert your value. What matters is direction—turning the energy of anger into constructive action instead of conflict. Work is not only a place to achieve; it is also a place to grow. The more calmly you respond, the more freedom you gain to focus on what truly matters.

**Anger and Relationships**

Anger often shows itself most strongly with the people we care about the most. Partners, friends, and family members are the ones we allow close enough to see our fears, our hopes, and our frustrations. When they disappoint or misunderstand us, the hurt cuts deeper. What begins as a small irritation can quickly grow into anger, not because of the moment itself, but because of what it represents—feeling unseen, unloved, or unappreciated.

In relationships, anger rarely exists alone. It often hides sadness, insecurity, or a longing for connection. Many arguments that seem to be about daily routines or forgotten promises are really about wanting to feel valued or respected. When anger becomes a pattern, it drains intimacy and replaces warmth with defensiveness. Both people end up protecting themselves instead of reaching out. Expressing anger is not wrong; it becomes harmful only when used to punish rather than communicate. The goal is not to avoid conflict, but to handle it with care.

Learning to express anger constructively means being honest without cruelty. Instead of accusing, describe what you feel. "I felt hurt when…" invites dialogue, while "You always…" builds walls. Listening is equally important. When someone expresses anger toward you, resist the urge to defend yourself immediately. Sometimes, people do not want solutions; they want to be understood. Listening fully can calm anger faster than an argument ever will.

Forgiveness plays a quiet but powerful role. It is not about excusing bad behaviour, but about freeing yourself from the weight of resentment. Holding on to anger is like carrying a burden that grows heavier each day. Letting go does not mean forgetting; it means choosing peace over punishment.

Relationships thrive when both people take responsibility for their emotions. You cannot control how someone else reacts, but you can choose how you respond. By calming yourself first, you create space for understanding. That space allows love to return after conflict. Over time, this becomes a cycle of trust—where anger no longer destroys connection, but deepens it through honesty and care.

Healthy relationships are not free of anger. They are built by people who learn to handle it with grace. Each time you respond with patience instead of pride, you teach your heart that love and anger can coexist.

ꙮ

# 13

# PATHWAYS TO HEALING

Anger is one of the most common emotions we all experience, yet it is also one of the most difficult to control. It often arrives uninvited, takes over our thoughts, and leaves behind regret once it passes. While a small amount of anger can sometimes push us to stand up for ourselves or take action, unrestrained anger can cause deep harm. It can damage relationships, ruin reputations, and erode our peace of mind. Healing begins when we finally stop justifying our anger and start asking ourselves what it is trying to teach us.

The first step toward recovery is simple to understand but difficult to practise—admitting that anger has become a problem. For many people, this admission feels like failure, but it is actually the greatest act of courage. It means you are no longer hiding behind excuses or blaming others. You are ready to take responsibility for your emotions. Once this awareness begins, genuine transformation becomes possible.

When people are under stress or feel threatened, they usually react in one of three ways: by suppressing their anger, by becoming defensive, or by lashing out. Each of these responses offers momentary relief but creates deeper problems in the long run. Bottling up emotions might look calm from the outside, but it is like trapping steam in a closed container; it will eventually explode. Defensiveness builds walls between people and prevents understanding. Lashing out damages trust and often leaves behind lasting guilt.

Learning to manage anger means learning to pause, to breathe, and to think before reacting. It means developing the ability to choose calm over chaos. This is not easy, but it can be learned with the right mindset and support. The goal is not to suppress anger but to understand it, to respond with awareness instead of impulse.

Recognising that you need help is not a sign of weakness; it is a sign of strength. Anger management counselling, therapy, or guided learning can help you become more aware of your triggers and teach you how to express emotions healthily. Everyone can benefit from these techniques, as anger affects every aspect of human life, work, relationships, parenting, and even self-esteem.

If you find yourself snapping at children over small mistakes or reacting harshly to situations that don't truly matter, take that as a signal to pause. Many of us yell, punish, or withdraw because we have never learned another way to express frustration. But anger does not make you powerful; it makes you disconnected. By learning new skills, you can start to rebuild the connection between emotion and understanding.

Anger affects not only your emotions but also your body. When you get angry, your pulse quickens, muscles tighten, and breathing becomes shallow. The body prepares for "fight or flight." Over time, this constant stress response can harm your heart, increase blood pressure, and weaken your immune system. You might find yourself exhausted without knowing why. These physical reactions are your body's way of telling you that something needs to change. Healing begins when you learn to calm both your mind and body.

A simple yet powerful exercise is to pause whenever you feel anger rising. Take three slow breaths, focusing on the sensation of the air entering and leaving your lungs. Feel your shoulders loosen. Let your jaw unclench. Remind yourself that this moment is temporary, and you have the power to choose how to act. The more you practise this, the more naturally it comes when you need it most.

Talking to someone you trust can also be helpful. Ask them how they see your anger. Sometimes, others can spot behaviours we overlook. They might tell you that you interrupt often, raise your voice quickly, or seem tense even in small disagreements. Such feedback can be uncomfortable to hear, but it is incredibly valuable. It gives you a mirror to see yourself clearly. Accepting feedback without getting defensive is one of the most mature steps you can take toward personal growth and change.

Counselling can help you take this awareness deeper. Therapy is not about judgment or punishment. It is about understanding. A good counsellor helps you explore where your anger comes from, what patterns keep it alive, and how to change your reactions. It is a safe space where you can speak honestly, release bottled-up emotions, and rebuild confidence in your ability to control yourself. Over time, this process creates not just calmness but also self-respect.

In the early 1970s, psychiatrist Aaron T. Beck developed what is now known as Cognitive Behavioural Therapy, or CBT. His discovery changed modern psychology. Beck realised that people's emotions are often shaped by the way they interpret events. When we assume the worst, we create unnecessary suffering. For example, if someone disagrees with you and your first thought is "They don't respect me," anger naturally follows. CBT teaches you to question those assumptions. Maybe the disagreement was just a difference in perspective, not an attack. This change in thinking leads to a change in feeling.

CBT helps people identify harmful thought patterns and replace them with balanced, realistic ones. It encourages positive self-talk, self-reflection, and better communication. Instead of reacting to every perceived slight, you learn to evaluate situations more calmly. Over time, this shift changes not only how you think but also how your body reacts. Your heart rate slows, your muscles stay relaxed, and your mind becomes clearer.

One of the reasons CBT is so effective for anger management is that it teaches you practical, repeatable skills. You learn how to express feelings without aggression, set healthy boundaries, and stay grounded in stressful moments. It includes techniques like assertiveness training—so you can stand up for yourself firmly but calmly, and relaxation exercises to quiet the body before anger builds up. When used consistently, these methods can completely transform how you deal with conflict.

However, no method works if you resist help. Many people avoid therapy because they fear being seen as weak or broken. In truth, seeking help is one of the strongest choices you can make. It means you care about your emotional health and the impact you have on others. It shows you are ready to grow. Therapy takes courage, honesty, and commitment, but every bit of effort pays off.

A strong relationship between therapist and client is essential. You must feel safe, respected, and understood. The therapist's role is not to lecture but to guide you through self-discovery. They help you look at your emotions with curiosity instead of shame. As trust grows, you begin to open up about memories, fears, or patterns that may have been shaping your anger for years. This openness allows healing to move from the surface to the core.

Through therapy, many people rediscover forgotten parts of themselves, like kindness, empathy, patience, or joy, that anger had buried. As these qualities return, you start to feel whole again. The more you practise awareness, the more control you gain over your reactions. You begin to notice anger rising and choose not to let it rule you. That moment of pause, that conscious choice, is the essence of healing.

Support from family and friends can also make a difference. The encouragement of loved ones keeps you motivated and grounded. When those around you understand that you are trying to change, they often become more patient and supportive. Their faith in you can serve as a reminder of why your effort matters. Healing is rarely solitary—it grows stronger in connection with others.

Over time, you will start to notice real change. Conversations that once turned into arguments may now end in calm discussions. You may find yourself listening more, apologising faster, or walking away when something is not worth your peace. These are quiet but powerful signs that your work is paying off.

Forgiveness plays a central role in this process. Anger often clings to the past, replaying old wounds and regrets. Forgiving others does not excuse their behaviour; it simply frees you from the burden of carrying it. Forgiving yourself is equally vital. Everyone has said or done things they regret. The point of healing is not to forget but to move forward with understanding. When you forgive, you make room for growth.

As your awareness deepens, anger begins to lose its grip. The same situations that once triggered you now feel easier to handle. You may still feel flashes of irritation, but they fade faster. You become calmer, more patient, and more thoughtful. What once felt impossible now feels natural. This is what progress looks like: steady, quiet strength.

Choosing to seek help for anger is one of the most powerful decisions you can make. It is not about weakness; it is about valuing peace over pride. Healing from anger is not about silencing emotions but transforming them into clarity, empathy, and balance. With the right guidance and consistent practice, peace stops being temporary. It becomes your new normal.

ᘓᘐ

# 14

# STRUCTURED LEARNING FOR ANGER MANAGEMENT

Very few of us can honestly say that anger never gets the better of us. The right trigger can pull even a calm person into a surge of emotion. A timely stitch truly saves nine. Learn the skills now so you prevent harm later. Structured learning gives you a map, a method, and the momentum to keep going when motivation dips.

Many employers host seminars or guest lectures because steady teams think more clearly, make fewer mistakes, and create safer environments, especially where deadlines are tight. Community organisations and non-profits often run free or low-cost classes that are open to all. These are easy places to start if you want to see whether a structured approach fits you.

Finding the right anger management course is easier when you know what to look for. Begin online and search for programmes that clearly describe what you will learn each week, who will teach it, and how progress will be measured. Read the facilitator's qualifications and experience with anger, trauma, substance misuse, and family systems. Look for practical elements such as skills practice, real-life scenarios, support between sessions, and a plan for what to do after the course ends. Ask for referrals from people who have completed the programme. Local listings and community centres can also point you to nearby options.

Enrolling can feel intimidating. Some people resist help because they fear judgment, or they hope the problem will pass on its own. Others have tried to change alone and feel discouraged. If you are supporting someone like this, you do not need to be their counsellor. Encourage one's first meeting with a professional and stay calm and consistent. For people who are in recovery from substance misuse or who have a history of aggressive outbursts, a structured programme is a safety tool rather than a luxury.

Once a person begins a credible course, progress often starts quickly. Early sessions focus on awareness of triggers, body signals, and the thoughts that fuel anger. Learners practise calm breathing, grounding, and simple thinking tools that help them pause before they speak. That sense of control is motivating. It turns learning into a personal investment rather than a punishment.

Home study can be a strong alternative. Privacy reduces embarrassment, and self-paced modules allow you to learn at your own speed. Effective home study still needs structure. Set a weekly timetable, keep a practice log, and test your skills in small, safe situations. Good syllabi include self-assessments, anger logs, reflection questions, and short drills. You study the nature of anger, identify your patterns, and rehearse skills without an audience. This can be particularly useful if you fear harming others during an outburst or if group settings feel overwhelming.

Strong programmes teach three layers of skill. First comes awareness, which means noticing early cues such as tight shoulders, a quickened pulse, or harsh inner talk. Second comes regulation, which means calming the body and steadying the mind with breath, movement, and focused attention. Third comes behaviour, which means choosing what to say and do so that the outcome is safer and more effective. Many programmes add communication skills, boundary setting, problem solving, and planning for difficult conversations at home and at work.

A simple lesson loop helps skills stick. Step one is notice. Write down the exact trigger and the first signals in your body. Step two is pause. Use one or two quick techniques such as slow exhale breathing, grounding your feet, a brief walk, or a sip of water while you count to ten. Step three is to choose. Consider your options. Speak now, ask for time, change the topic, or leave and return later. Step four is to act. Pick the smallest action that does the most good and the least harm. After the situation, review what you did, what worked, and what to adjust next time. Skills take root through repetition, not through theory.

Immersive seminars and retreats can speed up learning. A few days in a calm setting gives your nervous system rest and allow you to practise without daily pressure. Meeting others with similar challenges reduces shame and increases hope. You gather practical ideas, hear what has helped others, and leave with a plan. To make the gains last, schedule maintenance practices for the weeks that follow so the benefits do not fade.

Modern life is fast, and stress is common. Families can be shaken by one person's repeated outbursts. Denying the problem or sweeping it under the carpet usually makes it worse. The first step is admitting there is an issue. The next step is selecting help that fits your life. Choices include one-to-one counselling, support groups, short workshops, multi-week classes, online courses, and home study. Choose the format you are most likely to finish. The best programme is the one you complete and apply.

If you join a class, expect practical content. You will learn calm breathing, basic relaxation, and simple mindfulness to reduce reactivity. You will learn to challenge unhelpful thoughts and to communicate assertively rather than aggressively or passively. Many courses include light movement or yoga to discharge tension safely. Good classes show you how to let go of unhelpful emotions without denying them and how to direct strong energy into useful action.

A classroom can feel intimidating at first. Remember that everyone is there for a similar reason. Good facilitators create a respectful, non-shaming environment. You share only what you wish, and you focus on practice. Most people learn faster when they feel safe.

Choose wisely by asking practical questions. What are the goals? How many sessions? What practice is assigned between meetings? How will progress be tracked? What support exists if you miss a session? Is the programme suitable for your culture and values? How are safety and confidentiality handled? If legal or court requirements are involved, ask whether the programme provides attendance letters and compliant documentation.

Create a personal learning plan so your effort becomes a habit. Set two short practice windows each day, such as after breakfast and after work. Keep an anger log that records trigger, body cues, thoughts, action taken, and outcome. Use small drills, for example, two minutes of slow exhale breathing or a thirty-second pause before you reply. Invite a supportive person to be your accountability partner. Review your progress weekly and adjust one small thing at a time. Celebrate small wins, such as choosing to take a time out or asking for a calmer moment to talk.

Measure progress so you can see change. Track the number of outbursts each week, how long they last, and how quickly you recover. Ask a partner or colleague to rate communication on a simple scale. Compare your baseline after four and eight weeks. Improvement is often gradual at first, then faster as habits form.

Prepare for relapse since stress, illness, or life changes can reactivate old patterns. Write a short plan that lists your early warning signs, a person you will call, a simple time-out script, and a calming routine. If you slip, return to basics that same day. The goal is not perfection. The goal is shorter episodes, faster recovery, and less harm.

Structured learning adapts to many settings. Couples can agree to pause difficult talks and resume when both are calm. Parents can learn to regulate themselves first so that discipline becomes teaching rather than punishment. Workplaces can schedule brief skills practice in team meetings so that calm becomes part of the culture. Court-ordered people can learn the same core skills with added accountability and documentation.

Safety always comes first. If there is a risk of domestic violence, build a safety plan with a professional, identify safe places to go, and learn how to leave a heated situation early. Anger management is not a substitute for legal protection or crisis services. It is a skill set that supports safety and respect once immediate risks are addressed.

Digital tools can help you stay consistent. Many learners use reminder apps, smart-watch breathing prompts, or simple mood trackers. Others prefer paper planners and checklists. Use what you will actually follow.

When you finish a programme, continue with maintenance. Schedule monthly check-ins, keep a brief log, and refresh your core drills. New habits become part of who you are when you keep them alive in small ways.

There is no single perfect path. Commitment, practice, and support create change. Structured learning gives you a plan you can trust and the confidence to face difficult moments with steadier hands.

ജ്ഞ

# 15

# BUILDING A SUPPORT SYSTEM

Anger can be a real beast to deal with. It often begins as unresolved emotional baggage, a mix of frustration, hurt, fear, or insecurity that slowly builds up until it explodes in an out-of-control rage. Afterwards, you are left drained, ashamed, and wondering how things spiralled so quickly. The truth is that no matter how determined or self-aware we think we are, trying to handle anger entirely on our own rarely works. Even the most disciplined people need help, perspective, and accountability at times. And if you're not there yet, if you're still learning to recognise when anger is building up, don't worry. You're not alone in this.

This is where support systems come in, especially anger management groups. Think of them as a safety net designed to catch you before you fall too deep into your own reactions. In these groups, you meet people who understand what you're going through because they have been there too. You realise that you're not the only one who gets irritated over small things or struggles to calm down after an argument. Group therapy sessions are not cold, clinical spaces. They are warm, open environments built on empathy, where no one looks down on you for losing your temper. In these sessions, you can speak freely about what triggers you, hear from others about their own challenges, and learn effective techniques to regain control.

What makes these groups even more powerful is that they combine education with connection. Through guided discussions, practical exercises, and even humour, you learn to express anger safely, communicate assertively, and rebuild emotional balance. Many groups use creative methods to make the process enjoyable, such as journaling circles, relaxation exercises, or light-hearted activities to diffuse tension. Laughter, surprisingly, can be deeply therapeutic. It reminds you that anger does not have to define you and that you are capable of joy even in the midst of change.

For families, anger management sessions can transform the entire household dynamic. Imagine a home where everyone is quick to react: parents snapping after a long day, siblings arguing constantly, and children mimicking that behaviour. Over time, this environment breeds resentment and emotional distance. Family-focused sessions help reset that cycle. They teach everyone, from parents to young children, how to pause, listen, and communicate feelings before they boil over. Families learn to replace shouting matches with calm discussions and to resolve conflicts through understanding rather than control. The goal is not simply to manage anger but to change the way the family interacts and lives together. When everyone learns emotional regulation, home becomes a place of safety rather than tension.

The same principle applies to individuals or couples who decide to work on anger together. Joining a support group can make the process more encouraging and even enjoyable. It is not about suppressing anger; it is about transforming it into something that serves you rather than controls you. When approached with openness, anger management can actually be uplifting and rewarding. Some people join retreats or therapeutic camps designed around emotional well-being. These environments are intentionally peaceful, often set in natural surroundings, and include activities that restore both the mind and body. They may combine guided workshops with yoga, meditation, creative art, or nature walks. The goal is not just to learn about anger but to experience calm, perhaps for the first time in a long while.

For children and teenagers, such support can be life-changing. Between the ages of twelve and seventeen, emotions often run high, and anger becomes a way to assert identity or express confusion. Camps designed specifically for this age group blend learning with play. Teenagers get to talk about what frustrates them without judgment, meet others who share their struggles, and release tension through sports, team challenges, or art. These programmes teach them that anger is not something to hide or fear; it is something they can understand, manage, and express more healthily.

It is encouraging to see how society is becoming more aware of the importance of anger management. It is no longer reserved for people with so-called "problems." Workplaces, schools, families, and even churches are recognising that emotional health is a shared responsibility. Many organisations now offer group counselling sessions, workshops, and awareness programmes that make learning these skills accessible to everyone. Churches and spiritual communities, in particular, often play a meaningful role by providing group settings where people can reflect, forgive, and rebuild a sense of peace within themselves.

Of course, anger can still wreak havoc when left unchecked. In relationships, uncontrolled anger often leads to stress, emotional distance, and sometimes even violence. When one person cannot regulate their anger, the entire family feels its impact. That is why many people seek free or low-cost resources as a first step. If you or someone you know struggles with anger, reaching out early is essential. Start by talking to your doctor, who may connect you with a counsellor or local support service. Community centres often have group therapy schedules, while schools employ guidance counsellors who work closely with children showing signs of behavioural difficulty. In more serious cases, these counsellors can refer students to trained specialists for deeper help.

The internet is also a powerful resource. There are hundreds of websites that provide expert advice, downloadable guides, and even structured online anger management courses. These programmes allow you to learn at your own pace, often from the comfort of home. Many are designed by therapists and include interactive components such as reflection exercises or peer discussion boards. You can also find articles and videos explaining the science of anger, guided meditations, and tools for tracking progress. Whether you are an adult looking to take control of your emotions or a parent trying to help a child, there is tailored information available to guide you through each stage of the process.

For those who have already recognised that anger is becoming a problem, seeking help early makes all the difference. The sooner you acknowledge it, the sooner you can begin applying what you learn. Waiting too long allows anger to entrench itself in your habits, relationships, and thinking. With early intervention, whether through counselling, group sessions, or self-guided learning, you can break the cycle and start building a calmer, more balanced life.

Alongside professional help, reading remains one of the simplest and most effective ways to build awareness. There are countless anger management books written for different age groups and life situations, including children, teenagers, adults, couples, and families. Books for young readers often use stories and illustrations to help them name their feelings and recognise their reactions. For instance, a child might read about a character who learns to pause and breathe before shouting, and that image stays with them and helps shape their own behaviour. Teenagers benefit from books that address their specific realities, such as peer pressure, school stress, or emotional changes, and that explain anger in a language they understand. Adults can turn to books that combine psychology with practical steps, offering real stories and exercises that help change thought patterns. Couples and families may find books written specifically for relationship dynamics, focusing on empathy, listening, and compromise.

The challenge, however, is not in finding books; it is in using them. Simply buying a book and leaving it on a shelf does nothing. The real change happens when you start applying what you read. If a chapter suggests a technique for calming your mind, try it that very day. Keep notes about what works and what doesn't. Discuss the ideas with your partner or children so that everyone learns together. Over time, these small practices add up to significant improvements.

Interestingly, films can also be powerful teachers. Watching a movie that portrays a character struggling with anger helps us recognise our own patterns. When we see someone's temper destroy their relationships or lead to painful consequences, it hits home in a way that words on a page sometimes cannot. Movies make the emotional cost of anger visible, helping viewers understand the importance of change. Many anger management films also show the journey of transformation and how a person learns to confront their emotions, repair damage, and find peace. Seeing that process unfold on screen can be inspiring and can spark the motivation to start one's own healing journey.

Ultimately, the goal of building a support system is not just to control anger but to create a life where anger no longer controls you. It is about surrounding yourself with people, resources, and environments that nurture patience, understanding, and growth. Whether through group therapy, family sessions, retreats, online courses, books, or even movies, what matters most is that you engage with them actively. The tools you learn are only as powerful as your willingness to use them.

When you start seeing anger management as a shared journey rather than a personal battle, everything changes. Healing becomes easier. Growth becomes sustainable. And little by little, you transform anger not into suppression, but into understanding, strength, and peace.

ജ്ഞ

# 16

# THE PROFESSIONAL PATH

## Certification in Anger Management

As the world moves faster and becomes more complex, the pressure on individuals continues to rise. People today face constant demands on their time, attention, and emotional energy, and this often translates into stress and frustration. When this pressure goes unaddressed, it can manifest as anger. Across workplaces, homes, schools, and even digital spaces, the signs of poorly managed anger are increasingly visible. Recognising this growing concern, professionals around the world are stepping forward to learn how to address it effectively. One of the most promising developments in this area is the rise of certification in anger management.

Anger management certification programs are designed to train professionals in understanding, diagnosing, and guiding individuals struggling with anger-related issues. They are part of a growing field that merges psychology, behavioural science, and counselling. Companies, healthcare organisations, and even government agencies now understand that anger management is not a peripheral skill but a critical component of human resource management, public safety, and emotional health. Many businesses are creating dedicated wellness departments or partnering with professionals who specialise in this field to support their employees and create more harmonious work environments.

This shift has opened up a wide range of job opportunities for certified anger management counsellors. The demand for trained professionals is especially high in sectors where emotional control and conflict resolution are essential, such as law enforcement, correctional facilities, pastoral care, substance abuse programs, domestic violence prevention, and mental health services. Schools and colleges also require counsellors who can help students manage emotions and interpersonal relationships, while companies employ these specialists to mediate conflicts and improve communication among teams.

Anger management certification equips professionals with the knowledge and skills needed to help individuals and groups cope with anger in healthy ways. Through structured coursework, they learn techniques for identifying triggers, guiding self-reflection, and teaching self-discipline. Certified counsellors are trained to assess behavioural patterns and create tailored strategies to help clients replace destructive reactions with constructive responses. They also learn to manage challenging situations in therapy settings, where anger can surface unexpectedly, and to redirect that energy toward productive discussion and insight.

These courses often draw from multiple disciplines, combining elements of psychology, conflict resolution, mindfulness, and cognitive behavioural techniques. Professionals learn how to recognise emotional cues, facilitate dialogue, and help clients adopt coping mechanisms that lead to long-term behavioural change. They also gain tools for helping individuals understand the thought processes that fuel their anger, enabling them to shift from reactive behaviour to intentional action. In many programs, role-playing exercises, case studies, and supervised counselling practice help trainees develop real-world competence and confidence.

One of the major advantages of these certifications is their versatility. A certified anger management counsellor can work in diverse environments, from hospitals and mental health clinics to schools, rehabilitation centres, or private practice. Many professionals also provide online consultations or corporate workshops, which have become increasingly popular as workplaces adopt remote and hybrid models. Companies value this expertise because it not only improves emotional well-being but also reduces workplace conflicts, enhances teamwork, and increases productivity.

The presence of certified counsellors in schools and colleges is equally vital. Young people often struggle to understand their emotions and impulses, and unaddressed anger during adolescence can lead to lifelong behavioural issues. Certified counsellors in educational institutions help students learn to express frustration constructively, resolve conflicts peacefully, and build empathy. They serve as early intervention points, preventing anger from evolving into more serious aggression or withdrawal.

For those seeking professional help, it has become easier than ever to find qualified anger management counsellors. A family doctor or medical practitioner can provide referrals to certified professionals in the area. Many workplaces have mental health or employee assistance programs that include access to anger management specialists. Schools often have in-house counsellors trained in this field, and for those who prefer privacy, online platforms offer virtual sessions with certified experts who guide individuals through structured programs at their own pace.

Pursuing anger management certification can also be a deeply fulfilling career choice. The work combines compassion with structure, science with empathy. For those already in helping professions such as social workers, psychologists, therapists, educators, or life coaches, adding this certification provides valuable additional expertise. It expands professional credibility and opens doors to new opportunities in both private practice and institutional settings.

The rewards go beyond professional growth. Learning to teach others about emotional regulation often deepens the counsellor's own self-awareness. Many certified professionals report that the training not only enhances their ability to help others but also transforms their personal relationships and emotional health. Understanding anger from a clinical perspective allows them to handle stressful situations in their own lives with greater calm and maturity.

Because of the global rise in emotional stress and interpersonal conflict, anger management certification is now considered a highly relevant qualification. As awareness grows, more institutions are offering accredited programs that meet international standards. Graduates of these programs play an increasingly important role in building healthier workplaces, families, and communities. In a world where frustration and misunderstanding can quickly escalate into hostility, trained professionals serve as steady anchors of compassion and reason.

Ultimately, certification in anger management represents more than a professional credential. It symbolises a commitment to understanding human emotion at its most volatile and helping others transform it into strength. By teaching individuals how to channel anger constructively, certified counsellors not only change individual lives but also contribute to creating a calmer, more emotionally intelligent society.

ဢ

# 17

# ANGER IN THE DIGITAL AGE

Modern life has connected us in ways our ancestors could never have imagined. News reaches us instantly, opinions travel faster than facts, and our words can circle the globe in seconds. While this level of communication has many benefits, it has also given anger a new stage. The digital world has changed the way we experience, express, and spread anger.

In earlier times, an angry thought might have remained private or been shared only with a few close friends. Today, the same thought can be posted online for thousands to see. Social media has become a place where anger is easily triggered and quickly amplified. A single offensive comment or post can spiral into heated arguments and hostility. The lack of face-to-face contact often makes people say things online they would never say in person. Without the tone of voice or body language to soften meaning, even neutral statements can be misinterpreted, causing unnecessary conflict.

Digital anger takes many forms. It can appear as aggressive posts, sarcastic comments, long arguments in online forums, or passive-aggressive silence in group chats. It can also appear as internal frustration when scrolling through news that provokes fear or injustice. The endless stream of opinions, comparisons, and negativity can easily drain emotional energy. Over time, this constant exposure to online anger can increase stress, anxiety, and even feelings of helplessness.

Managing anger in the digital world requires the same self-awareness we use in real life, but with added discipline. The first step is recognising your triggers. Ask yourself what kind of online content or behaviour tends to make you angry. Is it political debate, misinformation, or personal criticism? Once you identify your triggers, you can make conscious choices about how and when to engage.

Before replying to a provocative post or message, pause and breathe. Read your words aloud before sending them. Would you say the same thing to someone's face? If not, reconsider your tone or your decision to reply at all. Silence can often be a far more powerful response than an argument that only fuels negativity.

It also helps to remember that online communication removes important emotional cues. People you disagree with on social media are still human beings with their own experiences and fears. Behind every harsh comment may be someone who feels unheard, hurt, or defensive. Practising empathy online may feel challenging, but it transforms digital spaces from battlegrounds into opportunities for understanding.

Digital boundaries are essential. Limit the time you spend on platforms that consistently provoke anger or frustration. Unfollow accounts that spread negativity and fill your feed with voices that uplift, educate, or inspire. Protecting your mental environment online is as important as protecting your physical one in daily life. You are responsible for what you allow into your emotional space.

For many, technology has also blurred the line between personal and professional anger. Work emails sent late at night, messages read without replies, and misunderstandings over text can easily cause resentment. Tone is easily lost in written messages, so clarity and patience are key. If a conversation feels tense, switch to a phone call or in-person meeting to prevent escalation. A calm discussion often resolves in minutes what could have turned into days of digital friction.

Parents today also face the challenge of helping children and teenagers manage online anger. Cyberbullying, exclusion from group chats, or arguments in gaming communities can deeply affect young minds. Teaching children to pause before reacting, to block rather than retaliate, and to talk openly about online experiences builds resilience and self-control. Just as we teach traffic safety, we must also teach emotional safety in the digital world.

There is also a positive side to technology. When used wisely, it can become a powerful tool for emotional healing. Online therapy, guided meditation apps, and digital journals can help people reflect, calm themselves, and express emotions safely. Communities focused on wellness and support can connect individuals who might otherwise feel alone in their struggles. The same medium that spreads anger can also spread understanding, compassion, and peace, if we use it with intention.

Anger in the digital age is not a new emotion, but a modern challenge. The principles of self-awareness, restraint, empathy, and reflection remain the same. What has changed is the speed and reach of our reactions. Learning to slow down in a fast world, to think before typing, and to choose understanding over outrage is the new form of emotional intelligence.

When we become mindful of our digital behaviour, we reclaim power over one of the most influential parts of modern life. Technology will continue to evolve, but our responsibility to use it wisely remains constant. Managing anger online is not about silence or suppression, but about choosing words that heal rather than harm, both for ourselves and for others who share this vast, interconnected world.

ജ

# CONCLUSION

## Reclaiming Your Calm, Reclaiming Your Life

Anger is a part of being human. It signals pain, injustice, frustration, and unmet needs. Yet when it grows unchecked, it can blur judgment, damage relationships, and leave lasting scars. This book has explored anger from every angle: its roots, its triggers, its physical and emotional effects, and the tools we can use to manage it. But understanding anger is not just about control; it is about transformation. It is about learning how to turn an emotion that once ruled you into one that now serves you.

The journey toward calm begins with honesty. You cannot change what you refuse to face. Recognising that anger has shaped parts of your life is the first act of courage. From there, awareness becomes your greatest ally. Each time you pause before reacting, you teach your mind that there is another way. You begin to see that anger is not the enemy but a messenger trying to tell you something about your needs, fears, or boundaries. When you learn to listen, anger becomes a guide rather than a weapon.

Real change rarely happens overnight. Like any skill, emotional regulation is built through practice, patience, and compassion. There will be days when you succeed effortlessly and others when frustration feels overwhelming again. Do not let those moments convince you that you have failed. Healing is not a straight path; it is a steady rhythm of falling and rising, learning and trying again. What matters is that you stay aware and keep choosing growth.

Self-compassion is vital on this path. Many people judge themselves harshly for losing control, saying things they regret, or repeating old patterns. But shame never builds peace. Forgiveness does. Forgive yourself for the moments when anger spoke louder than wisdom. Each time you choose calm over conflict, you are rewriting your emotional history. Every small step counts.

Managing anger is not about becoming emotionless or passive. It is about balance. It is about choosing strength over aggression, clarity over chaos, and patience over impulse. This balance allows you to express yourself clearly, stand up for your values, and still maintain peace within. When you master this, you are no longer reacting to life; you are responding to it with purpose.

Relationships often serve as mirrors for our emotions. The way we communicate during anger reveals how deeply we understand ourselves. Choosing to listen, speak respectfully, and set boundaries calmly not only improves relationships but also restores trust in our ability to connect. Healthy communication replaces the isolation that anger often creates. It reminds us that we are not alone in our struggles and that mutual respect can repair even long-standing wounds.

The modern world makes this challenge harder. Constant digital noise, social comparison, and online arguments can keep us in a state of irritation. But awareness of this helps. You can choose to slow down, disconnect, and create mental space. You can curate what you read, how you respond, and what you let into your emotional world. Protecting your peace in the digital age is not avoidance; it is wisdom.

Support plays a central role in sustaining progress. Whether it is therapy, a support group, a trusted friend, or a book that inspires reflection, every form of connection strengthens your resolve. People who walk with you on this journey help you see blind spots, celebrate victories, and remind you that change is possible. Asking for help is not a weakness; it is an investment in your well-being.

Anger management, at its core, is about reclaiming your power. When anger controls you, it decides your tone, your reactions, your relationships, and even your health. When you control it, you decide the quality of your peace, the strength of your relationships, and the direction of your life. True control is not suppression but understanding. It is the quiet confidence that comes from knowing that you can handle whatever arises.

As you move forward, remind yourself that calm is a practice, not a destination. Each breath you take consciously, each pause before you speak, each moment you choose understanding over aggression, strengthens the foundation of inner peace. You will begin to notice subtle changes: shorter outbursts, quicker recovery, and more clarity. These are signs that you are evolving.

In the end, anger does not disappear; it transforms. It becomes awareness, empathy, and strength. You learn that peace is not the absence of conflict but the ability to remain centred within it. You learn that forgiveness is not forgetting but freeing yourself from the past. And you learn that calm is not a fragile state but a resilient one, built from the quiet confidence of self-control.

If you have reached this point in the book, you have already taken one of the most important steps: you have chosen awareness. Now comes the real work—living these lessons daily. Remember that progress is measured not by perfection, but by presence. You are no longer reacting blindly; you are responding thoughtfully. That shift alone can change your life.

Take what you have learned here and build upon it. Keep a journal. Practise mindfulness. Talk openly. Seek help when needed. Forgive often. Choose calm, even when it feels difficult. Each time you do, you reclaim a piece of your life from anger's grip.

Calm is not something you find; it is something you create. It begins with one breath, one pause, and one conscious choice at a time.